road trip guide to the soul

A 9-Step Guide to Reaching Your Inner Self and Revolutionizing Your Life

Sadie Nardini

John Wiley & Sons, Inc.

Published by John Wiley & Sons, Inc., Hoboken, New Jersey
Published simultaneously in Canada

No part of this publication may be reproduced, stored in a retrieval system, or transmitted in any form or by any means, electronic, mechanical, photocopying, recording, scanning, or otherwise, except as permitted under Section 107 or 108 of the 1976 United States Copyright Act, without either the prior written permission of the Publisher, or authorization through payment of the appropriate per-copy fee to the Copyright Clearance Center, 222 Rosewood Drive, Danvers, MA 01923, (978) 750–8400, fax (978) 646–8600, or on the web at www.copyright.com. Requests to the Publisher for permission should be addressed to the Permissions Department, John Wiley & Sons, Inc., 111 River Street, Hoboken, NJ 07030, (201) 748–6011, fax (201) 748–6008, or online at http://www.wiley.com/go/permissions.

Limit of Liability/Disclaimer of Warranty: While the publisher and the author have used their best efforts in preparing this book, they make no representations or warranties with respect to the accuracy or completeness of the contents of this book and specifically disclaim any implied warranties of merchantability or fitness for a particular purpose. No warranty may be created or extended by sales representatives or written sales materials. The advice and strategies contained herein may not be suitable for your situation. You should consult with a professional where appropriate. Neither the publisher nor the author shall be liable for any loss of profit or any other commercial damages, including but not limited to special, incidental, consequential, or other damages.

For general information about our other products and services, please contact our Customer Care Department within the United States at (800) 762–2974, outside the United States at (317) 572–3993 or fax (317) 572–4002.

Wiley also publishes its books in a variety of electronic formats. Some content that appears in print may not be available in electronic books. For more information about Wiley products, visit our web site at www.wiley.com.

Library of Congress Cataloging-in-Publication Data:
Nardini, Sadie, date.
    Road trip guide to the soul: a 9-step guide to reaching your inner self and revolutionizing your life/Sadie Nardini.
        p. cm.
    Includes bibliographical references and index.
    ISBN 978-0-470-18774-6 (cloth)
        1. Self-actualization (Psychology) 2. Success—Psychological aspects. I. Title.
    BF637.S4N367   2008
    204'.4—dc22   2008017100

Printed in the United States of America

10 9 8 7 6 5 4 3 2 1

To you, my fellow traveler—may the road lead you forever home.

contents

introduction

The Trip of Your Life

my trip
The Day I Found the Road

The first road trip toward my soul happened before I'd ever been out of my small midwestern hometown. In fact, it was a one-mile journey to the gas station that changed my life forever.

I was in Iowa, trying to endure another winter night. I'd gone to college there for three years, hoping to figure out what I was meant to be, but so far wasn't having any luck. Not only was I not able to clarify my future plans, I was about to enter my senior year with no real plan at all.

One night, I was sitting in my car at a remote gas station, in the dark, daunted about opening the door because there was a "thirty-seconds-until-frostbite" skin-freeze advisory—and I'd forgotten my gloves. The temperature was eighteen degrees below zero with the wind chill, and I was miserable. My whole life felt like I did at that moment: cold, trapped in the dark, with no possibility of finding an easy way out of the situation.

Pumping gas with bare hands was out of the question, so in order to be able to buy some gloves, I wrapped my entire face in my scarf and, peering through a tiny slit for my eyes, I ran for the station's convenience store. I made it in fifteen seconds. Since no one else in the entire town was ridiculous enough to be riding on empty on the coldest night in recent memory, it was just me and an old man behind the counter. He must have been eighty. He looked like a farmer who was minding the store for a friend, but it turned out he owned the place. His name was Clyde.

Clyde looked up from his crossword puzzle, put a large weatherworn hand on top of his head, and said, "Where you headed?"

I sighed and answered, "I have no idea."

Clyde paused, then snapped his newspaper closed and used it to point at me. He said, "Well, you better get one, quick—you ain't getting any younger." He continued, unasked, as only the very wise—or very bored—do. "I waited to have an idea of who I was till I was seventy-five, and now it's too late. I wanted to be a farmer, but instead I ended up owning this here gas station for over thirty years. Same one I worked at since I was twenty. Funny how life works on you—when you let it." Then he squinted at me and said, "Wonder what it would be like if you put life to work *for* you, instead?"

Stunned, I returned home, realizing that Clyde was right. If I didn't follow my own heart and get to the work my soul was calling me to do, then life would do its own job on me. Before I knew it, I, too, would be stuck in a reality that didn't quite fit, like wearing my skinny jeans on a fat day. I would have a strange, seemingly random existence that didn't feel like mine. Without my direction, my life would become as unfocused as I was. I decided to make a move.

The first order of business was to leave Iowa. I'd been there long enough and wanted to see what other places held for me. But where would I go? I'd been hardly anywhere else. I didn't know anyone in another city well enough to rely on her help, and my finances were, well, collegiate. My mother, who by that time had been trusting the universe for years, said, "Well, why don't you just pick someplace at random, and wherever you choose, it will be the right one for you!"

I shrugged my shoulders and agreed. At least it was some sort of plan. So together we sat down at the kitchen table with a road atlas of the United States. Then she blindfolded me, to make me truly surrender to the magic she always believes is afoot. I set my intention strongly that the place I picked be the one that would serve me the best. I raised my hand over the map, with my index finger pointing straight down, poised to land. My mother spun the map underneath it. I took a deep breath and then put my finger down as I exhaled. I removed the blindfold with one hand, the other hand's index finger squarely on—Seattle.

I transferred to the University of Washington and moved to Seattle in the spring.

My new "make life work for me" process went like this: I intended, I put my heart into my goal, I trusted, and then I took action when action was required. In this manner, my life began to reflect my innermost desires. My moment with Clyde, and my application of his wisdom in my own reality, was a powerful first lesson on my road toward connecting with and moving from my soul at all times.

Now, nobody's perfect, and I still have my days of confusion. But no matter where I find myself today, I know I can make this moment into an intentionalized, heartfelt version of what I want my future to feel like. Then I offer it up to my soul and the collective soul of the universe to figure out how to bring this future to me in the best possible way. And it works, every single time. If it doesn't turn out exactly the way I thought it would, that's even better.

the map

With the map, you begin your own road trip to your soul—your true nature, and the future that's meant for you. When you learn how to connect to and live from this authenticity, you will have discovered life's biggest treasure: the road to a life filled with happiness and love. As I direct you along this road, I will reveal the ways to consciously guide your own living creation and become the person you know is inside of you, waiting to stop *waiting*, and start *becoming*.

Let's take a closer look at the word *becoming*. If "be" equals who you are right now and "coming" is something moving toward you and/or your moving toward something, then becoming is the result of your being, right now, what you want to be later. This is a major concept and one we will travel many inner miles to clarify. Without the mastery of becoming, you will continue on a road that is not your true path.

Using ancient wisdom from such Eastern disciplines as yoga, Zen Buddhism, Taoism, and feng shui, coupled with modern Western thoughts on science, mathematics, physics, and psychology, I'll show you where they all meet and point out to you the amalgam of universal wisdom you'll need to make your life a masterpiece. The road trip is, at heart, a process of becoming the most of yourself. So the purpose of this trip is to teach you how to let your soul become you, every day and in every way.

The map is meant to orient you to the road ahead, because it lays the foundation for the transformations you'll enjoy in all the other parts of your life. Once you've learned how the road trip to your soul works, you will be able to revolutionize any part of your present inner experience and make your outer world the best it can be. Whatever's gone wrong, you will be able to fix it and make it right.

You're on the verge of reading one of the most important keys of life, so you'd better be sitting down for this. What this book contains can shift you forever. You will learn a skill set that can give you back the power to be wonderfully, authentically *you* and have your life feel just the way you want it to. And really, at the core, what more could you want?

During the road trip, we'll visit nine steps or, as I call them, stops, together. Each of them is meant to transform another aspect of your life: your relationship to yourself and others, health, finances, letting go, and saying no properly, among others. Each stop contains crucial lessons you'll need to learn to succeed on your quest toward total evolution. Each stop has three major aspects that you should know about from the start. First, I'll share my trip with you, a story from my real-life travels. I'll describe the moment I had my own road-trip epiphanies so you can get the feeling we're going for. Second, information contained in the map section will bring your mind and heart into alignment with the teachings it contains. This alignment opens the doorway to your soul, or your connection to the greater source of knowledge that we all draw upon.

On this trip, you'll find out when to act and when not to. If you know when to step aside and let the universe—the soul's highest intelligence—do its work, then together you'll create miracles. I say "the universe" but you can call it love, possibility, inspiration, God, or the source of all creativity. You can call it hot pink if you want, but you are a singular expression of this energy, and it moves through you *as* you.

You will learn to allow this process to occur and not block it in any way. Allowing is trusting that you're doing the work to learn about and align with the person you wish to become, and now you can make space for that becoming to unfold.

Finally, with the "Take the Wheel" section of each stop, you are invited to move these teachings into action. When moments of opportunity come your way, you can seize them in ways that will bring major returns. You will learn to recognize the signals and signs that tell you action is needed and discover the specific moves that will get you where you want to go. Some steps are simple, some are challenging, but all are highly effective. I created each of them to have you zipping along your life's path by the time you finish this book.

Aligning, allowing, and taking actions to have the exact experience of life you want are the foundations of the road trip. In this chapter, you will learn how to navigate among them.

Again, the three steps to creating a joyful experience, or, as I call them, my Triple A, are:

- Aligning
- Allowing
- Acting

Yoga 101

Whether you can rock a handstand or have no clue what a downward-facing dog is, if you're here, you're doing yoga. *Yoga* means "union," and to do yoga means that you're drawing back into the wholeness of your truest nature. Specifically, you're uniting all aspects of yourself and then joining that whole self to the universal source that fuels you.

So many spiritual disciplines, including yoga, follow the three As. Alignment is what we do in our poses, in meditation, and with the breath, to line ourselves up with optimal energy. Allowing is when we trust the intelligence of that energy and let it heal and balance as needed. Finally, we take action, using our choices to refine our postures and also to live our practice more fiercely in the outside world. You'll learn to do this, too.

So many people spend their entire lives knowing that they are meant for amazing things, yet they live in a mediocre way at best. They go through their days hoping and striving for a better life, more money, the right relationships, less stress and worry. They work diligently in nine-to-five jobs, invest when they can, pay bills, and nurture their children into adulthood. Yet all the while they work and move through their routines, they feel a deep longing, a discontent. There's a hole inside that nothing seems to fill and a fabulous person stuck inside that hole who never seems to be able to get out.

Why do some of us seem to attract huge amounts of possibility, money, love, and bliss, while others feel continually blocked from it at every turn? Is it the luck of the draw? No, some people aren't magically blessed from birth. I think we each make or break our own luck. I've seen hundreds of clients turn their bad luck into good luck just by learning how to take charge of it. It's simple: the people who thrive have discovered the way to live, and they set about living. However, this takes education and practice to master. First, I'm going to share the basics with you, and then we'll deepen them at each stop along the way.

Know that your soul and its universal source want nothing more than to help you *become* your thoughts and feelings of greatness—to live within the boundless freedom and prosperity of the life you deserve. Abundance flows much more freely and easily than does lack. Love is a wider river than fear is. Like Clyde, you could always choose not to create your map and, like so many others, remain stuck at one level of the mind, always dreaming of the life you should have had and could have had, but never *did* have. I want to save you from that all-too-common fate.

You need a map to point you in the right direction, to revisit, to reorient you to your path, to show you the places where you've gotten off track, and to remind you how to get back on, fast. The map can keep you from becoming a statistic: one of the masses who live a good existence but not a great one.

It is also a guide to help you decide from one moment to the next how you can proceed with the most integrity as you move toward your goals. It may seem like a lot to think about, but once you live road trip–style for a while, you'll soon be able to do this with ease. You were born to delight in your life. Happiness is your right, and no matter how bad your life may have been, it's about to get much, much better.

The road trip isn't just about you, either. Any road to self-improvement should include awareness that what you're doing will affect your personal and world communities. With all the strife and discord today, it is our responsibility as one of the conscious collective to lead others by our example. To follow your map is to go first and show your loved ones how it's possible to live bright and large. Holding steady to your path shows others the way toward their own best lives. This is when the student becomes a master.

Gandhi said, "*Be* the change you wish to see in the world." He didn't mean later. He meant right now.

Science is now beginning to agree with this principle, and its findings describe what all the great philosophers, artists, innovators, and spiritual masters have known all along. Physicists have found that related subatomic particles, electrons, can react in the same way and seem to do so instantaneously regardless of being separated by a few miles. Quantum mechanics now says that what you observe becomes your reality, and that reality can *change*, depending on who is observing it and how. It's all in the perspective.

Science is coming around to the knowledge yogis have had for centuries: the quality of your energy, be it composed of intentions, emotions, or actions, can determine your reality. Your energy can be good if your thoughts, emotions, and actions are abundant and positive, but if you are being negative, or misaligned with what you say you really want, that quality declines.

Yogis and other masters take this idea further into the progression that by how you see your life and also by living in alignment with what you love, you will begin organically to open the doorway for the entry of the people and experiences that are like your being. In this way, without being detoured by what you don't have, you will start being all that you need—and this profound inner shift will cause your life to shift accordingly in the right direction. Once you know how to *be*, everything else falls into place.

Here are some of the road rules for you to follow as you progress through your road trip. If you remember them well, you will have the exact experience of life that you choose, every time.

1. Choose experience over things. The goal of the road trip, and of life, is to enjoy being alive in every possible moment. Instead of trying to gain only material items, like a new car or more money, you should primarily focus on *being* abundance, love, compassion, and alignment within. If you do this, the right stuff, opportunities, and people for you will present themselves, without your having to pursue them. I would rather be happy and in love with my life than have this exact thing or attract that specific guy if they weren't best for me—wouldn't you? If you desire to make a million dollars in one year and you focus only on that, you could easily miss the real riches of your life. Let the things you actually require, and lots of them, present themselves to you in the perfect amount—at the perfect time. Will you become wealthy, meet your soul mate, and have that beautiful house if you do the road trip? I can tell you that if you take the trip, and really *live* it, you have a damn good shot at them. And regardless, you'll fill that hole inside and live in joy.

2. Know your science. It is a common mistake among some scholars to interpret the emerging studies of quantum physics to mean that you can manipulate energy into any form you wish—that same new car, for example—just by what you think and feel, or that by focusing on something you want hard enough, you'll get it. Quantum physics doesn't dictate outcomes, and to claim it does is misleading scores of people into concentrating in the wrong place. In fact, quantum evidence shows the same thing that sages have said for centuries: people can change their *experience* of their moment by changing what they think and feel. You will be more successful if you concentrate on shifting your *inner* energy state to match the kind of personal and material wealth you want to have on the outside. Then, as physicists are finding, and since you see what you believe, you may begin to recognize more positive opportunities and

become more aware of possibilities that will take you to the next, higher level. Will you get palpable results at that level, too? Most likely, because when you are in internal alignment, you will tend to remove negative blocks to perceiving and accepting those more positive people and things into your life. Regardless, you'll feel good while doing it.

3. Release specific outcomes. Buddha said this a long time ago, and it still stands. It's not life itself that causes suffering, but *rigid expectations not being realized* that create great and unnecessary pain. If you await the arrival of specific things in a specific time, and you don't get them, and you get bummed out and trash your *inner* practice, then you have missed the point. Develop a daily saying: "May the best possible outcome happen for myself and all those involved." In this way, you remain in a high-consciousness, abundant state and trust that when you are in this state more often than not, the right outcome is assured. Predetermining what that outcome should be in advance will only cause you unnecessary expectations and the ensuing heartbreak of disappointment.

4. No outer blame, only inner responsibility. Just because you are a creator of your experience of this moment doesn't mean that you are at fault for all things that happen to you. This is a tricky balance, because how you've chosen to see and feel about your life has created a certain vibration that may make you susceptible to more positive or more negative outer experiences, depending on what attitude you broadcast. It often gets overlooked, however, that you are also dealing with other people's (sometimes unskilled) choices, and because of them, you may be in an environment that is not as healthy as it could be, a social system where you must make money and work and be responsible for others, and on and on. Things happen, and when they do, all that is required is to ask yourself if you

are internally in alignment, and, if so, you are again assured the best possible outcome. If you are not, do the work that's required to shift back into harmony, and make your own more skilled choices from now on. Stop blaming and get back to being.

5. Action *is* required: I want to stress that the road trip will work only if you take action when necessary. You must act to shift your thoughts, your feelings, your behaviors, and your choices toward what you wish to become. When I speak of the universe and its gifts to you, I am describing a bigger aspect of you, your highest awareness, which is responding to your cues. If you are not taking action, then the bigger you won't respond, either. So you'll learn to balance trusting the outcome with getting off your can and doing things to move closer to your very soul, rather than farther away. The power and joy of *being* is supported by *doing*.

To accomplish all this, let's take a closer look at the three As, your Triple A roadside assistance.

Aligning

Before you can create your life anew as you see fit, you must be aware that you created the way you feel about your life as it is *right now*. And because of those internal energies, you may have made choices and seen things in a certain way that affect your outside situation, too. You led yourself to this perspective, and you keep yourself here.

Within everything that is happening to you, positive or negative, you create your experience of it and you take actions around it.

Although you cannot make people do your bidding and have to deal with their choices, you have chosen to say yes to every one of the relationships, jobs, and responsibilities you now have. You have chosen every feeling you have about what you're going through. This is a shocking concept for many people to comprehend, so I'd like to get it out of the way in the beginning. It's difficult to come to terms with, and yet many of the great philosophies and spiritual traditions have expressed this idea.

I am not saying that you like everything that's going on in your life or that you are at fault for the things that have been painful for you, such as illness, abuse, or loss. I am not pointing the finger in an accusatory way or saying that you were always *aware* of saying yes, that you consciously chose your life to be as it is. I am, however, telling you that, whether consciously or unconsciously, whatever has been, and is, in your life, you are responsible for how you feel about it and/or whether you will continue with this feeling and these actions. And if you will continue, then how—this or some other way?

All that you feel is the result of your having aligned with, allowed, and acted out in your present reality. And that's good, because if you have a choice and you don't like your current circumstances, you can choose again and cross over the line between victim and master.

You exist somewhere on the line between totally positive and negative vibration, and, if you're like most people, you move around on that line from day to day. The problem is that so many people are not clear enough about who they are and what they want—or about their role as a creator—to manifest powerfully. You will soon learn to project your good vibes loudly and clearly and consistently.

The best news is that if you can really accept yourself as the creator of your present existence and know you've chosen the way you've experienced various scenarios of your past, then you have given yourself a huge gift. Consider this worldview:

- If you created your experience of reality, through the power of your mind, heart, and actions, then you must be able to create another reality as you wish.

- If you can create another, different reality, then you must be able to choose between at least two options and probably infinitely more.

- If you can choose which reality you wish to create, then maybe you could choose one that you really want this time instead of settling for less. Maybe you could choose to create an experience of your life that is so incredibly powerful, prosperous, and passionate, it will blow your mind.

Even by simply reading these words, you've just taken a major step toward changing your life, since your soul is yearning for expression. When you finally realize, as so many successful people have, that you are at the root cause of whether you love your life, even if you have to make radical changes to get there, and that you can make anything that happens to you a source of love, empowerment, integrity, and abundance *at will*, simply by changing your mind and heart, you will have made a major discovery. Put another way, as Matthew said in the Bible, "Whatever you believe . . . you shall receive."

Praying, envisioning, intending, desiring, asking, wishing, wanting, longing, dreaming—all are the same thing at the foundation. And that foundation is *frequency*. Your thoughts and your emotions—your most heartfelt intentions—are sent out from you in the form of a wave, like a radio transmission. Your desires are broadcasting directly to the energy field of the universe, your highest soul, and the cojoined souls of our collective consciousness, twenty-four hours a day. And because it is you, and it works through you, as you, it is also listening closely to the world you inhabit. So closely, in fact, that the specific quality and content of that broadcast you send out is *exactly* what you will get back as your daily experience of your life. You broadcast your heart out, and it comes back to you bigger.

The road trip contains powerful spiritual and personal wisdoms at every turn. However, there is only one main thing that you have to concentrate on: *be*—in love. At this frequency, you will attract the life you crave. The way to be in love is to immediately switch to a mind-set whereby you know that everything is already inside you that you require to be whole and happy.

An uncommonly great life is within your capacity, yet only when you let yourself burn as bright as you are will you experience total fulfillment. You can have tons of money, for example, but if you aren't happy, you won't be rich. So to become something—healthy, loving, respected, prosperous—you have to be it first.

Wherever your dial is set now, it's smart to do what responsible motorists do regularly: get a tune-up!

Allowing

As you revel in the power to create your life as art and take action, allowing the process to unfold requires your attention as well. To make the most of your trip, you must be aware that you cannot control everything that happens. If, in addition to deciding what you want to be and focusing your mind and heart on it, you also try to figure out exactly *how* you will make all of it come to pass, you will be a very unhappy camper, indeed. Because although you must take action when an action shows up to be taken, you cannot force the outcome by doing more, more, more. Many things in this process are not up to you. They are up to the universe, and even to other people's choices. If you make one outcome your everything, you block all manner of other possibilities. Journeying while locked into an itinerary can be detrimental to your trip, because there may have been a faster or more enjoyable route, but you didn't see it. No one else decides the direction of your life but you. But when it comes to receiving the optimal way, trust the process. When the way becomes clear to you, you'll know it, because it will light you up with excitement and rightness. Then make your move and take the required action.

The beauty of this is that when you feel frustrated that you can't make something happen, then you probably can't. Instead, lean back, let the process unfold, and turn to other areas of your life. You don't have to know all the answers. You only have to do the first part, the inner alignment, and take the positive actions you feel called to do. Then watch how the time opens up, a friend comes into your life, or the first opportunity knocks. No matter where it has to find you, it *will* find you. All you have to do is intend, feel, do the work at hand, and release the rest to the "it is all as it should be" folder. The more you can trust, as in any good relationship, the more beautiful your life will grow. Concentrate on making time to do your passionate creating, even for one minute a day. A single moment spent in connection with yourself is worth a hundred off-track ones.

By doing this, wherever you are, you will meet and recognize your soul mates: those people who step right onto your path to help you experience outside what you've always been inside. Usually, we don't even see them coming; it's as if they've been hiding in the bushes waiting for us. And it's true—you don't have to go looking. The ones who are at your level of resonance will be drawn to you even if you're sitting at your computer, hard at work.

To create your whole inner life to match your greatest vision requires a lot of will plus personal power, or willpower. You must be a willpower warrior to conquer your fears and move your life in a new direction.

Yet to allow is to also employ the opposite of action. It is to be *in*active on some levels of the process, so that your highest wisdom can become more active on your behalf. To allow is to cultivate the opposite qualities of action: softness, surrender, introspection, and waiting, as you trust that all will work out beyond your expectations.

By relinquishing any ideas about how your requests will be carried out, you release your grasp on any illusion of control, which in reality is only a way to constrict the flow of abundance. In yoga, we're encouraged to live in alignment yet let go of the fruits of our practice. We will enjoy them when they appear, but the real nectar is found in the moment of heartfelt presence we're cultivating. When things don't work out for us, we often think,

"If I only did more of this, then that wouldn't have happened." Well, the past is past. In your current reality, just *be*, in word, heart, and deed, more of *who you are right now*. Then if you're in alignment, and things don't go as planned, you can be sure that it wasn't right for you anyway and more easily move on. That's true freedom.

Just keep your hands on the wheel and your eyes on the road, and steer straight into being your vision. All else will be illuminated for you as you go.

Action

The final aspect to succeeding on the road trip requires you to put the pedal to the metal.

The word for *action* in Sanskrit is *karma*. Many yogis don't even know that only secondarily does karma refer to the result of past deeds, which are more properly known as the *phalam*, or fruit of your actions. So if you want good karma later, do good deeds now. You'll know what to do because good deeds are those that make you feel great. So you don't have to force yourself to be altruistic—you will want to be. You will get the chance to do what Buddhists call "right action" when you do what's best for your higher good and, therefore, that of those around you. Opportunities to do this will reveal themselves in the form of inspired next steps and invitations from others for you to do your life's work.

To fully experience the richness of the life you really want, when movement is called for, you've got to move. To accept the gift of a more positive life, with all it holds, is major, for it is to say yes to your worthiness, your vision, and your right to have the kind of abundance most people think is reserved for the very smart or the very lucky. You might be both, but you don't have to be either to be a success at life, or to reap its benefits.

How do you welcome the opening of a new existence? You do something about it. Accept that exciting new job offer. When that interesting person you ran into at the bookstore asks, "Would you like to have dinner with me sometime this week?" say, "How about Thursday?" When someone offers you a big check for your efforts, take it, cash it, and spend some of it on fun, some toward your responsibilities, and some to help the world.

Road Rule

If an opportunity makes you feel excited, happy, full of life, just say yes!

Part of being a success at manifesting your desires is to show up and do the work required of you, so when the next step appears, you'll be ready. If you're a painter, you need to start painting and finish your pieces, so when a friend brings a gallery owner to see your art, you have something there. You can passively allow the universe to do its work on your behalf even while actively doing your own work. The road trip is a working partnership between these two creative artists.

If you do not seize the opportunities that arrive, you become what yogis call *adharmic,* or out of alignment with your most powerful life path. It's more like walking down a side street or a dark alley when Park Avenue is just a few blocks over. To turn down an offer from the universe, by either saying no, ignoring it, or not getting the necessary work done, is to say, "I'm not serious about my vision."

Moving into aligned action each day is part of what makes you feel happy and whole. It will make you shine. That luminousity will then begin to manifest more of itself into your life, affecting others around you for the better, and, before you know it, everything will get a whole lot brighter.

Road Rule

Use your thoughts to organize, your heart to harmonize, and your actions to *materialize.*

I've now given you all you'll need to be able to understand the foundations of your trip. Before we continue on to the nine stops of your life, I'd like to offer you some simple yet powerful techniques to move these concepts into action.

take the wheel
Create Your Personal Map

Now that you've learned the necessity of having a map, you will next begin to center in on what you want your life to look like. Start discovering your present answer to the eternally asked question "Where is my life going?" with these next two steps.

Step 1: Refine Your Life's Design

In yoga, the fine tuning we do within each pose has a major pay-off. It helps us open the body's energy flow so we may enjoy a higher quality of life and healing. We call it refining, and you can use this technique, too.

You may know the obvious answers to the question "What do I really want?" Most people desire some combination of the following: money, love, romance, health, happiness, and success. But I want you to go further and be as detailed as possible. If you wish to draw into your heart and life *exactly* the experience you resonate, then you'd better know your intentions exactly, and in advance. The more room you leave for interpretation, the more you may receive surprises you weren't planning on or consciously wanting.

For example, let's say you desire a great romance, but are only being a more romantic person half the time, and the rest of the time you say, "This is lame," forget your practice, and veg out on the couch for hours, boring even yourself. Then—surprise!—you attract someone who is romantic at first but who then ends up on your couch with the remote control permanently attached to his hand. If you want a partner who is able to sustain romance throughout a primarily positive long-term relationship, and whom you also love in return, then you should be asking unequivocably for that by acting like that even when no one is around to see. Try to avoid personal characteristics or exact dollar amounts. You're looking to list specific energetic and heart qualities of any outer situation you desire, so that you can emulate them internally.

Take your time. Your diligence during this part of the road trip will pay off—big time.

If you need more inspiration, ask yourself the following questions:

- What are my passions? These are the things that, when you're involved in doing them, time itself seems to stop.

- When am I happiest? Doing what and with whom?

- What would make me even happier than the way things are right now?

- If I had all the money and all the time in the world and no one I was responsible to—you might want to sit with this scenario for a while—what would I do with my life?

- What does my perfect day look like? This is a powerful exercise, so write it down, tracking that day from waking in the morning until bedtime, and then see how your current life aligns to it. What would you need to be and do differently to make that day possible?

As you go through the process of refining who you want to become, double-check your list. Make sure it is geared toward what would make you truly excited to be alive. "I want my bills to disappear" might not be as heartfelt as, "I want to make enough each year to feel rich—to be debt-free, with lots of money left over for travel, fun, and freely helping others in need."

Step 2: Align Inside

After refining the structure of a yoga pose, we then encourage ourselves to expand within the new space we've created, filling the container with our hearts and souls. In this way, each bundle of arms, legs, and torso transforms into a vehicle within which our spirits can ride. So if you want something, you've got to start making room.

When you detail your descriptions of what you want in your life, you will then have a map to show you how to be. If you don't exist in inner harmony with what you want, you send a signal that you're not that serious about your request. In that case, you're likely to receive a more lukewarm version of your desire, if any. Those who send out the clearest, strongest message reap more benefits. You will then act like a homing beacon so your manifestations will know where to find you. You'll become like a lighthouse, to guide your universal gifts safely to your door.

To do this, you must commit to doing the next two practices for at least forty days, the time yogis and scientists alike say it takes to truly break old habits. Of course, you will continue the process of manifesting throughout your life, but the first push must be the most intensive, to uproot old belief and practice systems and replace them with new ones.

The next two exercises will help you instantly retune your mind and your heart to a higher frequency. Optimally, do them in the morning, and you will see a corresponding shift in the rest of your day. Whenever you come up against a mental or emotional block, do the second technique, the Inner Teacher, to find the source of constriction and open it.

My Incredible Life Meditation

The purpose of this meditation is to get your mind and heart to attune to right being. The more specific you can be with your vision and the more deeply you can feel it in your heart, the more effective it will become.

1. Begin in a comfortable chair or lying down.
2. Breathe deeply and slowly through your nose, pausing for a moment after each inhale and exhale. Let your rib cage flare out on the inhales and contract on the exhales.

Concentrate your attention on the sound and sensation of your breathing.

3. When you feel more centered and relaxed, begin to create a scenario in your mind of a moment in the perfect day of your most incredible life. Perhaps you're standing on the terrace of your mansion looking out at the sea or having dinner at your rustic country house with good friends. Whatever your grandest vision is for your future, see it right now.

4. Begin to notice every detail of your experience, and once you can see everything clearly, begin to bring your vision into the feeling realm. Spend as much time as you wish on each sense. Spend the most time on your heart feelings.

   * Start with touch. Pick up objects; feel them, their texture, temperature, and weight.

   * Move on to smell. Are there aromas? What are they? A fine wine? Fresh flowers? Salt air? Breathe them in deeply and feel the pleasure they cause.

   * Then listen for the sounds that accompany your future. Can you hear seagulls outside? The laughter of a lover and friends? The clinking of silverware? Great music?

   * What about taste? Roll that fine wine over your tongue. Enjoy the flavors of the meal in front of you, or perhaps taste the brine of the sea as you look out over a pink ocean sunset.

   * Finally, and quite importantly, begin to feel all of these aspects of your experience at the heart level. Your vision should be so good, so hugely abundant, that it brings a smile to your meditating face and joy into your heart. Feel every great sensation this vision brings you now. Experience love for those around you, delight in all that you have, and feel glee that you have become the person you dreamed you could be. The bigger the good feelings in your heart, the better.

5. As you exit the meditation and slowly open your eyes, keep your vision in your heart and stay with the feeling of happiness for as long as you can. Let it guide your actions. Throughout the day, return to your vision, or create a new aspect of it that's exciting to you. Keep returning to your vision whenever you need to shift back into the expanded state of your own possibility.

The Inner Teacher Technique

If, while considering your best life, you feel confused, blocked, or otherwise negative, and you can't seem to figure out why, rest easy: you already have the answers. In yoga philosophy, we call this the Inner Teacher, the source of our deepest knowledge. Each person has the ability to connect to his or her soul's library and become the ultimate authority on what he or she needs most. With practice, you can learn to access your Inner Teacher at will and begin to direct your next move from a place of authenticity and purpose. This relationship will revolutionize your life.

Here on the road trip, we'll do a three-part technique that will show you how to find out that you actually do know what at first it seemed as if you didn't know.

Step 1: "Har" Clearing. If you were driving on a country road and a huge oak tree had fallen across the whole path ahead, you wouldn't ram your car into it again and again—you'd call someone and have the obstacle removed.

Since you've come upon an energy block, it is just as necessary to reset your mind and body back to a clear place before you try to go any farther inside. To do this fast, you will need to balance your thymus, a gland located in the upper part of the chest just behind your breastbone that directs your body's healing and immunity. The thymus is also known in Chinese medicine, acupuncture, and yoga as a major energetic crossroads that effects change in your central nervous system and other pathways of the body.

Anytime you feel intense or negative emotions, fatigued, or off balance, you can do a clearing. It's easy:

1. Make a fist with one hand. Place it on your chest just below the notch at the base of your throat.

2. Inhale deeply and pound firmly on your chest nine times. Each time you do, exhale in a short burst and say, "Har," striking the roof of your mouth with your tongue on each *r*. This is a vibratory sound used by yogis to promote emotional stability. The vibration is also thought to stimulate your pituitary, another master gland of your hormonal and energetic balance. When you say "Har," press in your navel to make your exhales quick and strong. Let your inhales happen naturally in between.

3. Now you should feel more calm and centered. The negative feeling in your chest should have lessened. If it hasn't, repeat the sequence two or three more times. Come back to this technique whenever you have something you want to clear away from your path.

Step 2: Ask Your Teacher. Now formulate a question about why you're feeling a block around this issue. The general template is: "Why do I feel [insert your negative emotional state] when I'm thinking about [what you're asking for]?" If you feel anxious while envisioning a romantic soul mate in your life, you might say, "Why do I feel [anxious/afraid] when I'm thinking about [being fully loved for who I am]?" Write down this question at the top of a piece of paper. If you're literally on the road, a diner napkin or a matchbook will do. Writing can help clear your mind so the Teacher will appear.

Step 3: Receive. Usually when you have a problem, you try to think hard to solve it, right? To get the answer you seek from your Inner Teacher, you don't need to chase after it. In fact, the more you reach for it, the more elusive it will be. Your Inner Teacher does not like to be pressured. To access your deep wisdom, you must learn the art of inner listening: get quiet, be patient, release your grasp, and *receive*.

Have your question in front of you, then close your eyes. Simply listen for five minutes. Your mind will fill up with lots of chatter at first. That's okay. Let your thoughts play, and wait for a wise new voice to appear—a message from the teacher. Soon you will begin to get ideas, inspirations, and messages straight from your soul. Trust your Inner Teacher's wisdom and try not to rationalize it away. You'll know a good answer because it will ring true in a way that deeply calms you. A good gauge is: if you feel compelled to write it down, it's worth considering.

If you don't get anywhere after repeating your question three times, start free-form writing. Put down anything that comes to mind in response to your question, without forcing an answer. See what comes up in your mind or heart. Early memories are at the root of many a blockage, so recall how your family handled this issue—what defining moments happened to you, relating to it? What can you remember causing pain or fear when this subject came up when you were younger? When you intend to receive, you open yourself to the flow of your true understanding, and these epiphanies can take you to the next level.

In time, dialogue between you and your Inner Teacher will be like having an easy conversation, and the answers will be but a few seconds away. Even the act of asking and being open for the answer will start to dissolve the blockages, which cannot remain in the face of curiosity and willingness to change.

Your Life Shrine

In many cultures, home shrines—from the Latin *scrinium,* or box—are used as daily reminders of what one wishes to honor. Often used for religious purposes, shrines are also powerful when you use them to focus and honor your life's best intentions.

What is it that you want? Get creative: cut, paste, draw, and place meaningful symbols of what you want to include in your special place. Add candles for illumination and a jar of earth for staying grounded through the process. Let your shrine be both an inspiration and a constant reminder of why you do these practices. Look at it often in its beautiful, magical spot. Reflect on what it would feel like to have all that you see. Soon—perhaps sooner than you think, in ways that may surprise you—you will.

Say Thank You

As you move into the road trip, remember to say thank you. Gratitude is one of the most simple, hugely transformative allies you have to bring abundance in all forms to your doorstep. At all times, even and *especially* those that are difficult, scary, or challenging for you, find something to be grateful for that is already in your life. Find some aspect of the person you're with or the experience you're having that you can appreciate, no matter how small. This will expand your perspective and bring the energy of compassion back into the moment.

You'll become more able to navigate around potential arguments, stress, and highly emotional times because you won't keep looking at the area of lack, but will see what's good, what's possible, and what you can be thankful for. Then, no matter what you have to deal with, you will walk through it with grace and integrity.

Make a list of things you are grateful for. Whenever you need to, read it until you start to smile. There is no more beautiful contagion.

The Road Trip Begins

Now that you've laid down the road upon which to drive, and you've gotten your final destination in mind, at least for starters, we can begin the *Road Trip Guide to the Soul* in all the other areas of your life. So hop in and get ready for some excellent adventures!

the garage

Tune Up before You Ride: Tools, Quick Fixes, and Necessities for Your Trip

my trip
The Dreamfield

I was driving across Iowa, marveling that the place seemed to have even more corn than Nebraska. It was the Fourth of July, around dinnertime, and the roads were empty. As the rows of corn ticked by, I suddenly realized I hadn't smiled, said anything, or had a moment of fun in about 120 miles. That's because I was alone, with no one riding shotgun, no one for me to talk to or joke with. I felt terribly needy. Being alone made the past too loud, my fears too amplified. I wanted some company, even the unfunny-joke-telling, annoying backseat-driving kind. When I was alone, I usually would call on a friend or a lover to come and entertain me, amuse me, and free me from my terrible solo-ness. But I had no one in Iowa: I lived thousands of miles away and my cell phone service was spotty in the area. This was going to be a long, boring, lonely, slightly panicked day. Or so I thought.

As a last resort, I put an audiobook CD in the stereo, figuring that the least I could do was to pursue something intellectual while in my lackluster state. I'd never heard of the book: *The Santa Land Diaries* by the comedian/writer David Sedaris. I'd grabbed it out of desperation at the last Cracker Barrel store, wanting a voice to keep me company—anybody's would do. Sedaris began by describing his trials and tribulations while working as a Christmas elf for Macy's Santa Land over the holidays (he's Jewish). I laughed so hard I had to pull over. I was stunned. I hadn't expected to laugh, much less snort. And it had been as simple as paying $4.99 and pushing Play.

I decided to continue creating my own good time to see if I could break my addiction to needing company.

The moment I made up my mind to discover what adventures I could have all by myself, my cell phone rang. It was my best friend, Alexandra. At first I thought she would be the perfect cure for my loneliness. Alex is a choreographer and one of the most interesting people I know. She always has the best perspectives on my life, she makes me laugh, and we talk about crucial life issues, such as in which episode of *Sex and the City* was Mr. Big the most handsome.

I was just about to press the talk button, when I paused. I remembered the brief feeling of empowerment I'd had earlier. I hadn't yet begun to see what else I could do on my own.

I'd had at least three long-term relationships built solely on the desire to have someone else divert my time and energy away from myself, and, boy, did it ever work. Drama and dysfunction are great ways to turn one's attention away from one's own life's path. But so are fun, friends, and relying on others to fill the space inside my heart where I could have, and often should have, become more self-reliant. Friends and good times, support, and love from others are all important. But as my thumb began to pull away from the cell phone and I saw the call was going to voicemail, I understood that it was just as important that I get to know myself, fill myself up, and be able to stand alone—independently of anyone else. I'd neglected the other half of the equation for too long. And my sense of self was suffering for it.

After a few more miles of introspection, I pulled into Dyersville, Iowa, to search for the equivalent of a home-cooked meal. As I was walking down the road in search of a diner, a procession of festive Fourth of July locals walked past me, proudly adorned with red, white, and blue plumage. They waved and yelled at me to follow along. On a whim, I hurried to catch up and joined their informal parade.

We turned past a farmhouse into a clearing ringed by a cornfield. Families were seated on bleachers, on blankets lifted from couches and recliners at home. My parade friends separated in clumps of twos and threes, filling into the spaces in between. The place looked familiar to me. It was rather surreal when the fireworks started, and there, surrounded by pink- and green-lit flashes eliciting "Ooohs" and "Ahhhs," I realized I was sitting in the Field of Dreams—the one from the movie! You know, "If you build it, they will come"? The big, black Iowa sky was a perfect backdrop for the show. I leaned back and basked in the pretty lights, smiling, my boredom totally forgotten.

My goal had been to rely on myself that day—listening to and learning about me and what I needed. I didn't just follow my dream—I *made it happen*, like all my dreams since. I built it and, there in the clearing, I came to know my own potential to create soulfulness, all by myself, with no one's help but mine. I breathed in the pleasantly acrid air and sensed a distinct strength seeping into my heart, a feeling I would find ways to re-create on many more future days, anytime I needed to get back to *me*.

When I called Alex back later that night, she wanted to know if I was okay, since I'd left her a message the day before complaining about my loneliness. "I'm doing more than okay!" I exclaimed. "I'm with me."

This stop will give you some necessary tools to use along your way to keep yourself in a positive state of maintenance—and mind—when you're rolling along. You'll also find a few quick fixes for the times when you're stopped dead in your tracks, unsure of where to go next. Let's open the garage door, and look inside.

the map
Soul Fuel and Other High-Octane Fillers

Physicists and philosophers, yogis and masters alike have followed the road trip teachings—of the cosmos, the earth, and the hearts of man—straight back to the soul. The path you choose for yourself will have an impact—on you, on those you love, even on people you will never meet. When you realize it is you who makes your life change and not life that makes you change, you can finally begin moving forward.

This seems like a pretty daunting responsibility, until you see that it can be really fun to create your life in the shape of everything you love. If you had the choice of eating a plate of rotten food for breakfast, one you know would make you sick all day, or going to your favorite restaurant with friends and having a wonderful meal, which would you choose?

The road to your soul is both a path you're on toward your future and a path that's already right here. Stay in the moment, and choose your present intentions, words, and actions wisely, which is the only thing you can do, because the past and the future are not happening right now, and only what you do right now makes any difference. Even though you're gearing up to live your future dreams, you still need to bring them back *here* with the choices you make. So stay in the moment at hand and decide how you want to be later in your most incredible life, then *be it now at all times*. The garage will show you how to do this on your own.

Your Road-Tripper Status

As a Road Tripper, you are a person who is on the road to learn to live, love, and create from your deepest connection point with the great source energy that surrounds you and also *is* you. I call this the soul.

You're now making the necessary preparations for your trip so you can remain firmly at this center place even as you begin moving toward your vision. Here in the garage you will find tools you can use to transform any situation or relationship and retain your inner strength no matter what happens. Whatever you're broadcasting now, you're about to move to a new bandwidth. Here you'll find everything you need to get started, begin the journey, and last till the end.

Alongside positive change, challenge appears. You will confront old fears, old ways of being, as you drive to meet your soul. Along the road to your best life possible, be prepared for delays. There will be potholes, irritating construction, and long stretches of open space where nothing seems to be happening. That's life, imperfectly perfect. These lag times and frustrations are necessary to hone your discipline and commitment to your path. Just as it takes time to get your physical body in shape, it takes time to build new spiritual muscle, and it takes time to make your heart resilient enough to bear the fire of a fierce life.

Let's enter the garage and give you the tune-up you'll need to begin the journey that lies ahead.

Riding Shotgun

Calling shotgun is the ongoing battle to claim and then keep one's position in the passenger seat during a road trip of any duration. It is a power struggle, a battle of wills whose outcome is always uncertain, as other riders, even previously supportive family members or significant others, may use any available method to try to remove you from your rightful position.

A successful "I call shotgun" moment results in your sitting smugly, with radio, window, and glove-compartment rights for the time being. The feeling of power is immense. The position, however, is unstable. You are at the mercy of the driver, who has ultimate decision-making rights over your spot. The driver's seat is the only one that is constant and assured. The driver is the ultimate road-trip creator, navigator, and final decision maker.

Why? Because the driver is at the wheel, and it's hers to steer wherever he or she wants.

In this way, when you rely on an external thing to make or break your feeling of worthiness—whether it's a relationship, a job, community status, or more money; or you allow outside circumstances or people to dictate how you feel about yourself—you can be just as easily kicked out of the seat of happiness.

Let the first lesson of the garage be that you do not need anything outside of yourself to give you permission to be who you want to be. If you let others' visions entirely become your own, or allow their decisions to hold authority over your joy, then any feeling of solidity, acceptance, or power can dissolve as quickly as it was bestowed upon you. This happens because the happiness or stability was dependent on someone or something out there—and not on you. These feelings were nothing but an illusion, since the real, sustainable joy can come only from within. When you choose to hand over your wheel and ride shotgun, it can easily become giving your power away. Even the most loving person will not be able to sustain you forever, for that would drain them too.

Road Rule

You give your power away the moment you look to someone outside of you to validate any part of your existence—your worth, your direction, or your dreams— to the point where you override your own capacity to do it.

Handing Over the Wheel

Luckily, giving your wheel away isn't permanent. It's like offering a handshake—when you turn around and leave, your hand is still attached to you. Your power is like that—it's an inherent part of you. You can, however, choose to feel as though you've lost your connection to it, which creates a state of weakness, reactivity, emotional chaos. It's known as disempowerment, and it doesn't feel good.

During your trip, you will be much happier if you can keep yourself in the driver's seat as much as possible and steer away from calling shotgun in other people's rides. It may feel like a relief to let someone else drive, and at times you will do this. But if you ride passively for too long, people will always take you where *they* need to go, in the end. It's nothing personal; it's simply the nature of the soul to compel each of us toward our own final destinations, no matter how much we'd like to sit back and go along for someone else's adventure. We do intersect with other people's trips, often. We should share and delight in others and allow them to help and support us. But you cannot go everywhere with them or hope to find your own road if you're not willing to take the wheel meant especially for you.

Visiting the garage allows you to tap into your inner source of strength at will. To do this, you must do three things:

1. Create space in your life for the trip.
2. Hold that space each day through your focused intentions.
3. Practice new habits through action that add up to your new life.

If you're going to be taking the time and effort to travel through all the stops, you must do so with a clear idea of where you're going. Who wants to be driving on someone else's highway, when your own is so much more *you*? Remember your list from the map, of your life's vision? This is your first step toward making it happen in your lifetime.

Your Tool Box

You can use the following tools to help you along your chosen road, whatever it may be. They are guides for where to place your mind and heart while journeying inside. I will explain their concepts first, then later, in the "Take the Wheel" section, you'll learn action steps to employ your tools to help quick-fix any emergency road trip situation.

Tool #1: You

There are certain things and people you don't need, now or ever, to be successful and happy on your life's road trip. What and who they are may surprise you:

- Your loving husband, wife, or partner
- Support groups of any kind (not even your book club)
- Your concerned mother
- Your children
- Your best friend
- Siblings, cousins, first cousins, mothers-in-law. Even first cousins in-laws' mothers-in-law
- Basically, anyone besides you

It's not that you shouldn't have these people around; enjoying lots of healthy relationships is necessary for balance in your life. It's just that you ultimately don't need others—their support, their acceptance, their good moods, or their understanding—to do the work you came here to do.

When I say you have to go on this trip solo, I mean it. Even I can go only so far with you. You can receive help, advice, and opinions all you want, and you can welcome them into your life. But eventually, if you really want to make changes within yourself, you have to do it yourself. Reflecting on others' perspectives and suggestions is fine, but in the end, you will only gain the driver's seat if you jump into it, regardless of what anyone else outside of you decides to do. Take everyone else's opinions on your process both into serious consideration and with a grain of salt. In the end, only you know what is right for you, because only you can see into your heart and make decisions that will benefit it. And as all great masters have agreed, what makes you truly happy is ultimately best for all those involved with you. Honor your relationships, but don't forget about first enriching the foundational one you're building with yourself.

Tool #2: Tell, Don't Ask

Change can make people weird. They might start to act strangely when you change, even those who are supportive of your decision. Even you will sometimes react in ways that seem to contradict the changes you want to make. Why? Because everyone has two major aspects of the mind that fight against each other. Your conscious mind knows what's best for you and rationally wants you to make changes for the better, but your unconscious mind freaks out at the mere suggestion of doing something differently. This mind is preoccupied with keeping you alive, and since you're alive now, then you should change nothing for fear of death. It's irrational, yet is an old-school defense mechanism that exists nonetheless. If you want to make changes, even good ones, your unconscious mind is going to try to stop you through doubt, fear, resistance, and counterproductive behavior.

Knowing this in advance can help you recognize the feelings and actions your unconscious mind may produce around shifting into new ways of being. Use your rational, conscious mind to keep yourself on track, and soon your unconscious mind will relax when your new habits become your daily habits.

Others around you also fear change. It's often unconscious also, so try to realize that even if they don't. Be compassionate and reassuring, but hold your ground. If you truly want to transform an aspect of your life, you cannot wait until everyone around you feels perfectly fine about it; that could take a very long time.

The thought of positive change can be scary. The *experience* of it, however, is exciting and rewarding, and it feels right. Lead the way through your actions for yourself and your loved ones, and when you succeed, they will be amazed at what you have managed to accomplish and may want to get happier and healthier the way you did. So as you go on the road

Road Rule

The word *shift* is gentler than *change* and won't trigger the unconscious as much.

trip, you won't ask if you can change, you'll *tell* everyone that you're shifting into more of yourself.

I'm not suggesting you ignore other people's needs during this time, only that you make your focus strong enough, so it cannot and will not be wavered by outside dramas.

The road trip to your soul is ultimately about you. At the same time, reassuring the people around you will not only make them happier, it will help them to provide you with the space you need to do your inner work.

The main thing to understand about your loved ones is that all they really want to hear is that they matter to you and that you're not going anywhere. They will be more supportive of you when they know that the reason you're trying to change isn't because you're unhappy with them or losing interest, but that you cherish the relationship and want to be a stronger partner in it *with them*. However, too much concern about reassuring others can take you away from your own work. It's up to you to balance a firm commitment to what is right for you with staying in tune with the feelings of others and doing what you can toward achieving harmony.

By maintaining your direction, you'll show your loved ones, over time, that it's going to be okay, by doing what you know you must do to be truly in love with your life. Wouldn't you want them to do the same thing? The benefit of positive change is a two-way street: they get the best of you and so do you. On the road trip, what you offer to yourself, you also offer to your community and, therefore, the world. When you hop into your own driver's seat, everyone wins.

Tool #3: The Mini-Stop

The mini-stop is a simple way to open a window to your soul. You don't have to spend hours in concentrated practice to get there. Instead, take just a few seconds or minutes to pause, notice what's beautiful about your surroundings, and really take them in. This teaches you to remain alert to the magic surrounding you, and soon your life will seem to fill with potential and fun, because you know how to stop and look for it. Choose the "longcut," a mindful walk through the park instead of your usual rush, or catch up on one more chapter of a wonderful book. Sit in the café and write for a few moments instead of getting your coffee to go. Look up at the sky.

After finishing these sentences, I paused and let my gaze wander around my office. I noticed a quick movement outside my window. Now, I live in Brooklyn, New York, and my view is very urban—a fire escape and the brick building across the street. Nature shows up around here in the form of sidewalk-potted trees or the occasional dog on a leash. Imagine my delight when I glanced up from my computer screen to see a blue jay peering in at me. I hadn't seen one since my childhood, and my heart fluttered in delight.

I'm glad I didn't ignore what could have been just a shadow in my side vision, but had stopped to receive. It took only ten seconds, yet now I have a memory to cherish—and to share with you.

Life is sending you messages and simple pleasures all the time. It is constantly showing you the way to wake up and enter the stream of pure awareness. In this place of open eyes and hearts, everything becomes clearer. So make a mini-stop whenever you can and invite in the inspiration of now.

Tool #4: Soul Appointments

Each week, expand on the mini-stop and go soul-o, making time each week for a longer personal adventure.

Have you noticed that a yoga class is easier to skip out on than, say, a doctor or dentist appointment? Most of us think that time for ourselves can wait, which means we're undervaluing our alone time and, therefore, ourselves at a deep level.

You're with yourself twenty-four hours a day. It's like a marriage, only closer. Just as we tend to take our longtime partners for granted in some ways, we figure that *we're* always around, so taking time for ourselves is sometimes not the highest priority. We say it is, but our actions often prove otherwise.

Too much giving of your time and energy to others and your responsibilities, without putting back nourishment into yourself, will quickly drain you and negatively affect all other relationships in your life. When you say, "My time is not as important as everyone else's, and neither is replenishing my balance," this imbalance will manifest as your reality, as chronic fatigue, resentment illness, and anxiety. You will never seem to have time for yourself and you'll be off balance, yet you'll be giving to everyone else. It's a common thread among people who are nurturers and givers by nature. It's also a vicious cycle—one you can begin to end today.

This week, write in your calendar—in pen—a soul appointment with yourself. It should last at least an hour. Keep it as sacred and nonnegotiable as you would a business meeting with an important client. Doing this sends a message to you, your loved ones, and the universe that you are committed to your well-being, that you value yourself as highly as you do anyone or anything else. Others will then begin to see the value in you even more, because there is now even more value inherent *in you*.

These appointments are a step beyond the time you already spend with yourself, such as driving to work or cooking dinner for the family before everyone gets home. The soul appointment is special because you will do only those things that are soul food, which will increase your life energy. During this time, you will get to know yourself better, deepening your internal dialogue and receiving insight and inspirations that you could more easily overlook during the rest of your week.

Go somewhere that gives you joy, quiet, a few laughs, a much-needed rest, or whatever you require most at the time your appointment arrives.

take the wheel
Road Trip Relationships

Embarking on your road trip is for you and you alone. But you will want to communicate to your family and friends what you're doing, so they can in turn give you the space and time you require to really take your trip in a quality way.

Living in the now requires that you let people clearly know your intentions, without saying too much. It's your process, but it will affect others, so go ahead and relate. When talking about the road trip, you do not have to over-explain yourself. This can be hard, if you find creating boundaries and keeping energy for yourself to be difficult tasks.

Road Rule

The more words you use, the less energy you keep. When you speak, aim more for a haiku than an epic.

Here are a few relationships you may have, and how to handle sharing the road trip with them in one minute or less.

Kids. It's extra hard to concentrate on yourself when children are in the picture. For the trip, you'll need time to reflect, which means you must have some time alone. Choose your adventures and self-study to coincide with their naptimes or school days, or get a babysitter to help you make the space you need. If you have a partner, enlist his or her help to give you even an hour a day to nurture your commitment to yourself.

Kids understand what they've experienced, such as going to school. When you feel it's time, let the kids know that you're in school, too—self school. They'll want to know what it's about, and you can say, "It's where I learn to be the best of myself so I'm happy and can be the best possible parent to you." Let them know they're important and that they can help you by giving you study time like they have. You will let them know when "school's in," and they can give you the space and time to do whatever your homework is for that day.

Be firm with them and really take the space, even if they don't want to help or they act out. Hold your ground. This teaches kids that learning about oneself, and how to take one's life work to its highest potential, is a lifelong course of study and an important one to respect.

Adults. Keep it short and sweet. Any more than a minute or so of explaining yourself begins to move you more into a seeking-acceptance mode, and you may not get that right away. Think of it as a haiku: something powerful that can be expressed in just a few lines. Say something brief and clear, listen to their response, and then respond succinctly.

Be compassionate; as you decide to change things, even if others seem angry, judgmental, or hurt, or they try to subtly undermine your efforts. Stay unwavering and calm, showing them that you may be shifting but your love for them won't be. Once you have an understanding of one another, suggest going out to a nice dinner or something else to reassure people that they're still important to you.

Downers. Downers are a subset of adults who try to take you down every time you feel like going up. We can feel sorry for Downers because they must not like themselves very much, or they're scared. Only very insecure or frightened people can't honor others for their accomplishments, period. Whenever you change, expect to hear negative comments—sometimes from the people closest to you. Anyone can jump on the Downer train for a moment, including you!

If someone says something that's meant to let the air out of your tires, don't waste your precious energy on it. You know by now that wherever your attention goes, it will strengthen whatever it's focused on. You don't want to give a Downer any more power. My advice? Ignore them, period. You don't owe these unskilled comments any more of your time. If you ignore the Downers, they will either go away or shift into more constructive ways of dealing with you. Just don't let their bad choices work, and they won't.

Explaining yourself will only make you sound defensive and expend your energy; it will not change their minds but only gives Downers more fuel for their opinions. Excuse yourself, and move forward.

Emergency Roadside Assistance

The road you're embarking on is a powerful one. At times, it can be exhilarating and filled with epiphanies, and at others, you may get lonely, overwhelmed, or feel you can't go on. I know I just told you to go it alone, and the majority of the time, do that. There are, however, times when strategically reaching out can help. Just do it mindfully, in a way that doesn't undermine your efforts to self-center.

Breakdowns happen to all of us, and they can slow you down or even stop you in your tracks. They also begin to turn your perceptions toward your fears. It's natural to feel upset sometimes. But if you're wallowing in your emotions all the time, they can begin to create the opposite of what you want. It's best to meet a breakdown head-on, using the following tools, and to get back onto the road as soon as you can.

In order to stop the mudslide of negativity, the first thing you should do when confronted by difficult thoughts and emotions is to call Triple A. Go back over your map and see which of the three As—aligning, allowing, or acting—you are either resisting or not practicing in full. When you recognize breakdowns for what they are—momentary pockets of fear and resistance to living the life you really want—you will more easily put them aside and get back behind the wheel. After all, even feeling like giving up is just a feeling, not your master, and you can use some of the following tools to help recognize a breakdown, then realign yourself. This practice of putting things into perspective by yourself first will make you stronger.

Breakdown #1: The Flat

You felt like a million bucks when you met that cute guy or girl last week. He or she took your phone number—then didn't call. Now you're spending your precious evening sitting by the phone, waiting for it to ring. Your sense of strength and purpose dwindle with each second that ticks by, as if the ringer is connected directly to your self-esteem.

The Fix. Realize you're letting someone else's behavior dictate your happiness. Then pick up that same phone and call someone who cares. If you turn away from what's making you feel bad, and toward what will make you feel better, you'll regain your sense of strength. It tells your soul you will not run toward negative or distancing people for acceptance. Ask your best friend to meet you somewhere fun. Then unplug the phone from the wall, and get up, get dressed, and get out of the house. Go to a place that makes you remember how good it is to live, instead of waiting to feel alive until someone else decides you will. Remember the shotgun seat? Step out of it, walk around the figurative car, and get back behind the wheel. And while you're at it, thank the universe for saving you a whole lot of trouble by revealing someone who doesn't vibe with you. Hey—maybe your fun place even has people you can flirt with, and who will flirt back. There *are* others, you know.

Breakdown #2: Sugar in Your Tank

Everything was going so well. You decided to lose some weight and became committed to a healthier lifestyle, and now you're fifteen pounds lighter. Awesome! Then, perhaps something happened to stress you out, or maybe you just got nervous about how well things are going. So you and your subconscious just spent the evening frantically making up for lost time with your old buddies Ben and Jerry. You feel bloated and full of self-loathing, and want to throw in the towel altogether.

The Fix. Know that everyone backtracks sometimes. But it's over now, if you choose it to be. Don't make it any worse than it is right this second. Immediately, let the past be the past and make more constructive choices in your brand-new moment of now. Remember, your emotions will hear you when you say, "I'm so fat and terrible," and you'll get more of those feelings.

Instead, change your mind immediately, before the inner critic gets a chance to do more damage. Give yourself a break and realize that change is a balance of the majority of your actions over many days, not some kind of constant perfection—*no one can do that.*

Make a switch: go dance the night away or play a pick-up basketball game with your buddies to burn it off—your solution should happen ASAP, to remind you that rebalancing is just a decision away.

Breakdown #3: Coolant Leakage

You meant to make it to yoga class but somehow found yourself screaming at your sister on the phone. Now you missed both the workout and the bliss, and instead you got stuck in the same old family dramas that always were dead-ends and always will be.

The Fix. Final-curtain the drama. Hang up (respectfully), turn around, take a bow, then step off the stage. Walk out to your car, say to your imaginary public, "Thank you. It was so nice just to be nominated." Then drive straight to the next yoga class. After the bliss takes effect, call your sister back and say something nice, even if she doesn't. Keep it up, balancing space with compassion until the reactivity has faded and you can communicate again from a place of gratitude for who you are to each other.

Throw Out Your Broken Tools!

When you reach for a tool to help maintain your balance, make sure that what or whom you reach out to will help you get to where you want to go, not hold you back. Ten after-work beers instead of two? That doesn't solve anything; it just covers the problem that will come back later, in some other, bigger way. Or reaching out to your joysucking ex-girlfriend in a time of need? Not the best idea.

Dependency-promoting tools are instantly gratifying, but they stunt your growth and cause other issues to sprout up alongside the ones you already have. So using them doesn't assist you in the way you want them to. They actually *add to your problems.* Read that again. They add, by upsetting you and those who care about you. They attract more of the same into your life. Over time, they can make you physically ill, stressing everyone out further. This is not about guilt; it is a study of choices, and the effects of those choices. If your goal is to deal better with times of strain, of self-doubt, and of fear, then replace your broken tools.

Swapping your more destructive, ineffective coping mechanisms for powerful ones that help you deal with your dramas, gets them to lessen instead of build up, and makes people you love happier as a side effect is a very, very good tool to have at your disposal. Here are a few other tools I suggest keeping in your garage.

Speed Dial

If you could press a button and get instant access to feeling much better about yourself, while your stresses melt away, would you do it? I would. It's called "speed dial," and on the other end should be between two and four people who know you well, love you unconditionally, and, most of all, make you laugh.

The dialees are not to be overrelied upon, since you want to build self-reliance, but called into action right when you need them most. Find something in town that sounds fun to you, maybe *only* you, then call your carpool buddies and go. You may not want to get up, but to break out of a bad funk, it helps to have a change of venue.

Newton's second law of motion states, "The rate of change of the momentum of a body is directly proportional to the net force acting on it, and the direction of the change in momentum takes place in the direction of the net force." In other words, when you want to make a positive change, you must do something positive to get moving in the right direction.

Newton isn't aware of this, but his "force" is sometimes known in modern times as "getting off your keister." Whether it's going to dinner in a fun place or just meeting on a park bench to talk, a proper carpool will gladly meet up with you, as long as they know it's helping their friend into a happier state of mind. You'll feel better soon; you just have to make the right move.

Jump-Starters

These tools have the uncanny ability to uplift your mood in mere seconds. They're simple, and quite obvious, yet many people veer off into habitual drama ruts when a more constructive solution is right in front of them.

All you need to break an emotional cycle is to introduce something that makes you laugh, hope, feel thankful, or dance. Have a more fun, life-affirming experience, and you will feel much stronger, no matter what you're dealing with. To invoke the flow of life in your favor, you must first change your mood. Give yourself five minutes to wallow, then grab a positive tool. Have these tools at your service in advance, so you can employ them as needed for any and all breakdown moments:

- That romance novel you stopped (on purpose) just before the bodice-ripping part, or any great book or magazine that diverts your attention (yes, the *Sports Illustrated* swimsuit edition counts).

- Break out the covert collection of cheesy movies you're ashamed to admit you own but can't wait to watch.

- You bought yourself a gift certificate to your favorite store or salon. It's good for one of the following: power drills, lingerie, car parts, furniture, bikini waxes, or a new hair color. Now go cash it in.

- Compile a hand-pasted and decorated "My Trip" scrapbook containing photos and mementos of all the people, places, and things that remind you how great your life can be, and that you're loved.

- Make a CD of your top-ten favorite road-trip tunes of all time. Then play them. On repeat. As many times as it takes to make you dance.

- Write "A Love Letter to My Favorite Person"—from you to yourself. Mean it, then seal it in a beautiful envelope and open it whenever you need a boost. Then write another one to have around for later.

Your Getaway

When it comes to wanting space, we may not like it when other people ask us for it, but we all need it. Creating space around yourself, especially at a moment's notice, is an art, and one you can begin to think about beforehand. Virginia Woolf beautifully described this personal hideaway or private moment alone as "a room of one's own."

I think your getaway can be anywhere you feel inspired, calmed, and creative. It can be somewhere you go to think alone or a place you can enjoy with people you love. For me, it's a neighborhood pub in Brooklyn with speakeasy decor and a great jukebox. It's a place that's seen a lot of life, which inspires me to examine mine, and enough smart, interesting people to encourage my slowly improving struggles with the *New York Times* crossword puzzle.

We all need a private relationship with ourselves and a room of our own where we could read a magazine and eat jelly doughnuts if we wanted to or ponder life without distraction. Sometimes you need to do what you like, when and where you like. You must be in a safe, clear state of mind and heart to do the work of living your dreams, so when you need it, go out and get it.

Take this week to search for your getaway. It might be as close as your bathtub or far across town. It can be quiet, loud, anything you wish—perhaps the sound of Monster Truck pulls allows you to think. Just find your place, go regularly, and keep it to yourself.

You might sometimes choose a getaway where you go to volunteer. It can be a children's cancer ward, the Humane Society, a care center for the elderly, a maternity ward, a community garden project, or a homeless or abused women's shelter, or you can become a Big Brother or Big Sister. Volunteering enriches your community and in return you gain perspective of what's really important in life.

Road Trip Diary

Buy a journal and take a moment to write down a list of the tools that will work best for you. Create new ones—whatever will help keep you on the road in times of resistance and doubt. Put down your immediate thoughts: what struck you about this chapter and what you feel you could do to make some changes in your life, starting today.

You don't have to wait until you break down to visit the garage and take out your tools. They're great confidence and independence builders, too. In fact, practicing maintenance now will help you avoid more energy drain and emotional storms later. Spend some time each week at your getaway. Make a soul appointment— and keep it. Get that silly movie—and watch it tonight.

Now that you've got some tools under your belt, perhaps you'll feel more confident about going on the trip. Actually, you're already on it. Gearing up for the journey is just the beginning. As you move farther down the road, and on to new adventures, remember that although you go it alone, you've got a whole community of road trippers traveling down the highways and byways all around you. Welcome to the road trip. We're all in it together.

the gas station

How to Fill Up with Soul Fuel and Keep from Driving on Empty

my trip
A View to Remember

When the morning sun came up over New Mexico, I almost crashed my car. I'd never seen a landscape like that before: all rolling sky and gnashing rock teeth worn smooth from tasting centuries. When the sunlight hit the cliffs, it instantly seared them the blood red of passion.

I was twenty-two, on my first road trip out of the Midwest, where it was so flat that if a tornado touched down, news stations in five counties started getting eyewitness calls. I'd hardly seen a hill, much less what looked to me to be a mountain on fire.

It occurred to me that if I was going to continue staring at this phenomenon, I might want to stop driving at the same time. So I pulled onto a scenic overlook, got out, and glanced over at my fellow gawkers. There were two other cars parked there, and both drivers were alone, still in their vehicles. As I passed between them, I could see that the man to my left, who was wearing a business suit, was talking on a cell phone, looking down at what he was writing on a notepad, and the woman to my right was looking in the rearview mirror, chin tilted up, putting on her mascara. They didn't notice as I walked over to the railing.

For about five minutes, I stood, taking in the marvelous colors. There were subtle yellows and oranges dancing on the hills in the bonfire of sunrise, and the guest appearances here and there of green desert plants and tiny purple and blue flowers, final touches on this masterpiece of nature.

I developed a warm feeling, almost as if the new sun was hitting my body and making it warm and red, just like the view ahead of me. As the sensation spread to my hands and feet, I was aware that what was happening was a renewal of my life energy. I'd been so mindless lately—working too hard and not making time for myself. I wasn't eating right and could not remember the last time I took a bubble bath instead of a quick, I'm-late-for-work shower.

I marveled that the only thing I had to do to refill my soul was to get out of the car and stand there in appreciation. With my heart open to the experience, and my head's tendency to be cynical or ten steps ahead of myself taking a backseat for a moment, I was able to simply receive.

When I'd had my fill, I walked back to my car. The two others were still in theirs, he still on the phone, and she now on to lip liner. Did they ever stop and look at the wonder waiting for them through their windshields?

I was often that person, so caught up in my daily responsibilities that I forgot to look around me, and to intake soul fuel in the forms of beauty, art, laughter, and joy of living. I know so many people are, too.

As I drove away from the overlook, my left foot kicked something solid, and it rolled under my accelerator. I reached down and retrieved it, and saw it was a rock small enough to fit in my palm but big enough for me to see how unique it was. On top, it was plain, the color of sidewalk, definitely nothing special to look at. But on the bottom, it was entirely made of clear crystal points, and all the facets sparkled in the daylight. It made tiny rainbows on my dashboard.

I put the rock in my shirt pocket, smiling, and looked at the clock. I didn't have a lot of time, since I was going to meet a friend. I was actually a little late. But because I decided to eke out those five extra minutes for myself, I have a lifelong memory, and more than a few people have been inspired by it. I was ten minutes late to meet my friend, yet because of my story, she decided to go to her first yoga class that day—and now she's a popular yoga teacher who, in turn, gives hundreds of people a place to rejuvenate their bodies and minds.

And the rock? Well, a few years later, I gave it to someone who needed it even more than I did. Besides, I remember its lesson well, and whenever I need it, I can feel it here, as always, sitting next to my heart.

the map
Fill'er Up!

Yogis call that which energizes us *prana*. Chinese healing masters call it *Qi* or *Chi*. European philosophers called it *elan vital*, or the "spark of life," and they equated it with the soul. Many people in the West know it as *life force, good energy,* or *vitality*. Here in the gas station, it's known as *soul fuel*. What is this energy that so many spiritual philosophies speak of, and how can you get more of it? Let's go back to Mother Nature for a clue.

According to science, *thermo* or *heat* means "energy in transit," and *dynamics* describes the movement of that energy. Thus, in essence, *thermodynamics* is the study of how energy moves and how movement itself is powered by energy. The language of thermodynamics was originally created to describe the mechanisms and efficiency of the steam engine, but it works just as well on you.

The first law of thermodynamics states, "The increase in the internal energy of a thermodynamic system is equal to the amount of heat energy added to the system minus the work done by the system on the surroundings." In terms of the soul, this law means that the increase of your life force is equal to the amount of energy you take in minus the amount of energy you give out. This seems pretty straightforward, but it's surprising how many people don't know how or neglect to balance this simple equation in their daily lives. The main issue is that for most of us, it is far easier to give energy away than to make the time and effort to replenish it.

Energy can be material, as in things you can see and touch, such as food, water, and vitamins. These physical forms of energy are often the main sustenance for individuals who are not making a regular practice of refueling the soul in other equally important, if not more important, ways. Material energy is necessary for survival, but it is one of the less energetic ways to intake *prana*. As in many spiritual philosophies, a good rule of thumb is that the more you can see energy, the less refined it is. Now, it's fine to eat, hydrate, and take your multivitamin. But to reach the highest levels of your being, you must also maintain a steady diet of what I call ethereal energy.

Material energy burns in your body in processes that transform it into heat, or pure energy. Food's energy, however, is mostly expended on the body. It is used to sustain you on the physical level: tissues, muscles, your brain. Ethereal energy comes in its high-octane original state, straight from the source. It is not seen but felt as love, excitement, or hope, it causes an often dramatic increase in aliveness that doesn't just fuel the body, it fuels the heart and the soul. We often neglect to feed the energetic "body" as regularly as we do our stomach.

Many healing modalities see the roots of disease as an imbalance in ethereal energy, which eventually manifests as a breakdown of the physical body. Still, taking in destructive material energy in the form of low-quality food or unhealthy drink, or restricting the flow of health in the body through stress, anger, or other undealt-with issues, are all ways that have been well documented to cause an array of physical, mental, and emotional problems. That's because, in the end, we need both positive material and ethereal energy coming in and not expending more than we have to maintain an optimal balance. If one or the other side of the thermodynamic equation is lacking in you, and you're running on fumes, there's much more of a chance that you'll run out of gas.

On this trip, you have a unique invitation to transform many areas of your life at once. One of the main foundations for the progress you make on any level begins with the quality of soul fuel you're pumping into yourself each day. You simply must have premium life force existing in you at all times to be able to do the rest of your work optimally.

Road Rule

Fill up with *prana* every day—and never give all your fuel away.

Find the Fuel

In the gas station, you can self-generate a constant flow of energy that will sustain you through all your experiences and be there when you need it most. But it's up to you to continually refill your supply.

What exactly is soul fuel? Well, philosophers, spiritual leaders, and scientists alike have debated that for centuries. Some think it's a life force that enters the body in the form of breath. Some see energetic fields around all living things and think perhaps these fields are attracted by some combination of health and intention. Some believe we're born as energetic beings made physically apparent, and the life force is with us from the beginning. Scientists see moving energy as the foundation of everything in existence.

In almost all cases, however, the amount of life energy you have is thought to be changeable and susceptible to your thoughts, feelings, and actions. Yogis call this *pranayama,* or the practice of filling up with life essence. *Pranayama* describes the ability you have to direct the flow of energy, according to your intentions. Depending on what you think, feel, and do, you'll have more or less fuel in your tank on any given day. That's a powerful notion, that you can either be more empty or more full of life, depending on what you choose.

You don't need to know exactly what soul fuel is to know when you're low on it or when you feel more alive. You can probably even list the things that can drain you and other things that replenish you. Jot some down right now, and be specific:

Five Things That Drain My Soul Fuel and Five Things That Fill Me Up

Drains Me	*Fuels Me*
1._____	1._____
2._____	2._____
3._____	3._____
4._____	4._____
5._____	5._____

How many of each are you allowing into your days?

Many people list working too hard, feeling stressed, not taking time to relax, and having dysfunctional relationships as examples of what drains them, yet they continue to go through day after day engaging in exactly these activities.

What about the five things that most enliven you and make you feel joyful? Don't worry if you're not yet doing enough of them—I just wanted you to see your balance on paper. In the gas station, we'll concentrate on adding more energetic fillers to your daily routine.

Something to know about soul fuel is that other people want yours. And in fact, you probably want theirs, too. This can be a positive thing. We all exchange life energy every day in the form of conversation, paying attention, and offering love and support. Even looking someone in the eye and smiling is a way to offer it. A saying that exemplifies this is, "Where attention goes, energy flows."

Optimally, your close relationships should be ones in which the flow of ethereal energy in such forms as love, respect, sharing, and trust is roughly equal. Yes, you're giving a lot, but the other person gives back to you. You are never depleted by this type of interaction. Shakespeare described this type of exchange when he wrote, "The more love I give to thee . . . the more I have."

But many times, we find ourselves in situations that are characterized by negative energy drain, such as obsessive worrying, fighting, overworking, enabling, or any other situation where the person you're dealing with isn't giving his or her share and you are overgiving. Anytime you feel depleted after an interaction, you can be sure you've been soul siphoned. Just what caused it may not be conscious, but you'll know when it's happened.

The rule of thumb when dealing with energy flow in your life is that positive energy makes more life force flow in, and negative energy causes your life force to flow out. The cycle of soul siphoning benefits no one and diminishes the life essence of everyone involved.

It's great to get energy from other people. Yet it is imperative that you develop a consistent practice of refilling your tank on your own as well. Why? Because sometimes you may choose to give a lot when receiving isn't as equal: in a crisis, if work is momentarily overdemanding, if someone you love falls ill. You'll need a surplus of soul fuel for those times. Plus, if you can't do it for yourself, no one else can sustain you for long without being siphoned themselves. You don't want to overrely on externals for what you can and should be giving yourself on a daily basis. When you know how to fill yourself up, you will never again be without a supply of personal power.

Having an ongoing discipline of keeping yourself in an abundance of energy is necessary if you want to use it to accomplish your greatest dreams, have deep and meaningful relationships, heal old patterns, and participate fully in your life. If you're a giver, it might be an incentive to know that the more vitality you have, the greater you will be able to participate in more quality ways in all your interactions, and you will do greater things for your community.

Another meaning of *pranayama* is "to retain life force." This is a direct message that you can give all you want, but you must keep enough for yourself by drawing energy into your body, mind, heart, and soul continually.

take the wheel
Action Steps for Soul Fueling

Fresh fruits and vegetables, which contain living energy when you eat them, are more highly ethereal than most other foods. They are material, and healing for the body, but also provide you with soul fuel at a very refined level. Every day if you can, eat a large, vegetable-heavy salad. Try to make it as colorful as possible to hit the spectrum of nutrients and health benefits. Avoid lowering the vibration with foods that are not as alive, such as cheese (unless it's fresh, and made without binders or other junk), bacon bits, heavy salad dressings (instead, try balsamic vinegar combined with Dijon mustard, olive oil, pepper, and lemon juice), or croutons.

Add fresh fruits onto anything you can: breakfast cereal, yogurt, your salad, or, my favorite, apples with peanut butter, or just have fruit by itself. There are other living foods, too: yogurt contains healthy bacteria you need for good digestion.

Take a page from my Native American ancestors, and before you eat, thank the food for nourishing you and offering you its life so that you may live more fully. Then eat with reverence. This intention increases the healing resonance of your food. Then make of your life something great, something that honors all those beings that gave their lives to make yours possible.

Say Less, Fuel More

There's an old yogic saying: "Save your breath to cool your porridge."

How often do you speak words that aren't important to you? Do you engage in conversations that are mindless, or even detrimental, such as gossiping or complaining?

Too often, we overgive advice instead of simply listening. We talk out of boredom, nervousness, or insecurity. Any way you slice it, overtalking equals soul fuel siphoning. It's not merely the words; speaking takes focus and intention. If you are using that power to say things you don't really care about or that make you (or others) feel bad, then you will want to close your mouth and consider a more advanced practice.

Today, say only what's important. Listen more, be more quiet, talk on the phone less, and don't engage in lukewarm or petty conversation. If you're choosing to participate in conversation, that's saying yes energetically to it.

If you must say something, express it economically, then use the rest of your energetic savings to get back to all your grand road trip adventures. In this way, you, too, will save your breath to do the things that serve your higher purpose.

Let Your Breath Save You

A third meaning of *pranayama* is central to the practice of physical yoga postures. *Prana* also means "breath," and the practice of breathing in conscious rhythm with your intentions, and with nature, is thought to improve the flow of life force within you. Western science concurs, and many studies show the healing power of oxygen and calming benefits of deep breathing. You can think of it this way: breathing properly is pure soul fuel. The majority of people, however, actually breathe backward, reversing the benefits.

When you're born, your natural state is to expand your chest and belly on the inhale and contract your rib cage and belly on the exhale. To calm and balance your central nervous system, you must learn to breathe like this again. Often, as stressed-out adults, we either hold in the belly all the time or don't use it at all, and breathe shallowly in the upper chest. This type of breathing can actually cause an anxiety response in the body—we breathe this way when we're panicking.

On a scientific level, the following three breathing techniques have been shown to calm your brain waves and central nervous system within thirty seconds, which then stimulates your endocrine system to regulate the hormones of immunity, aging, metabolism, digestion, and health, among others. They are used by countless people to keep the life force flowing, the body healing, and stress to a minimum.

As a yoga teacher, I have seen firsthand the power of breathing properly. I will teach you to do it and, with a little practice, it will become first nature.

When you practice these techniques, keep your mind and heart working in concert with your breath. Your breathing won't be as effective if you're thinking about your terrible day while trying to calm down. Instead, on your inhales, think "love" or "my daughter" or "strength," something that feels good to you. On your exhales, simply feel that you're letting go of all negativity and worry. Let the inhales empower you and the exhales release what's no longer serving you.

The first technique I'll teach you is a foundation for all the others, and if you have to choose only one, let it be this one. Practice conscious breathing for at least two minutes per day or whenever you feel anxious. Do all three styles daily if you can. Put a sticky note that says "Breathe" on your computer, program your phone's screen saver to display it, and write it in dry-erase marker on your bathroom mirror.

The Setup

To breathe properly, you must first connect to your pelvic floor muscles, because if you let them go slack, you will not be able to take a deep breath. This adjustment also instantly wakes you up to lift and engage these muscles, by stimulating your central nervous system. In yoga, this action, coupled with drawing your navel in toward your spine, is called *mula bandha* (pronounced moola bunda), or "the root lift." It unlocks a powerful amount of latent energy stored at the root of the spine.

Not only yogis have learned to harness the huge amount of life force within the pelvic region—all great singers know that to cultivate the richest sound vibrations, they must activate the pelvic floor.

These muscles are found at and around the base of your pelvis, all intertwining like a freeway in Los Angeles. They connect your sitting bones to your pubic bone in the front and your tailbone in the back. For women, lifting these muscles gently feels like doing a Kegel exercise, and I'm told that engaging the pelvic floor for men is like urinating, then stopping the flow. It's a delicate area to talk about, but one of the most important—and underused—muscular and energetic areas to strengthen. Without a strong pelvic floor, lots of unwanted physical bills can come due when you're older, such as incontinence. Practice lifting these muscles as you breathe and they will become more resilient as a result. As a benefit, you will raise your energy vibration right away.

Ujjayi (Ooh-Jai) Breath

Also known as "ocean-sounding breath," this style of breathing is used in yoga classes throughout the world. Getting back to a more natural way of breathing is necessary for a balanced body and mind, and this technique has the added bonuses of strengthening your cardiovascular system and helping you find your soul's center in any situation. That's a tall order, but *ujjayi* delivers.

Once you learn this method, it becomes extremely simple to do, and you can do it anywhere.

1. Sit comfortably, either cross-legged on the floor or in a chair in a regular sitting posture.

2. Gently lift your pelvic floor muscles upward. Notice that doing so makes you sit straighter and instantly gives you

a feeling of more alertness. This position is the foundation around which you will breathe. Keep the muscles lightly engaged the entire time you practice.

3. Begin to breathe slowly and deeply through your nose. Since you're not active, you may want to pause for a second or two after each inhale and exhale so you don't become overstimulated by breathing too quickly.

4. Bring your hands to either side of your rib cage. When you inhale, expand your ribs out into your hands and breathe all the way down into your belly. When you exhale, keep the height you've created in your spine and the openness in your ribs, but contract inward at your belly and waist area. Your navel should draw more into your spine on each exhale. Think of inhaling more space around the heart and navel and exhaling by drawing in the navel and the side waist.

5. After a minute or so, let your hands rest with the palms on your knees or thighs. Continue breathing the same way, expanding on the inhales and contracting on the exhales.

6. The hallmark of the *ujjayi* breath, and something that may seem silly at first but soon becomes a benefit, is the throat action. Open your mouth, take a deep breath, and then exhale as if you're fogging up a window or a pair of glasses. You'll be constricting the back of your throat somewhat. See if you can hold that action and inhale through it, too.

7. Now, since this is a nose-breathing exercise, keep the sound but close your lips. You'll now be breathing through your nose, but the back of your throat still has the slight contraction that will make the "ocean-sounding breath" of which we speak. Not only does this action at the back of your throat help bring more breath and, therefore, healing oxygen into your bloodstream, it also makes your lungs, diaphragm, and abdominal muscles stronger.

That's because, much like adding weights to a bicep curl, you've added resistance to your own breath. And as we're learning on the road trip, we can use resistance to make us stronger.

8. Continue the *ujjayi* breath for at least two minutes, using slow, rhythmic cycles of three to five seconds for each inhale and the same on the exhale. You can increase your time to five minutes or even longer.

Using the foundation of the *ujjayi* breath you just learned, move on to practice the next two variations, each powerful in its own way.

Double Down

For panic attacks or other moments of anxiety, use the double down technique. This breath will calm your central nervous system, so use it whenever you feel an anxiety attack coming on, or anytime you need to soothe your body, mind, or heart.

1. Lie flat on your back on the floor or a bed, if possible, for the most relaxation.

2. Using the same *ujjayi* technique described in the previous section, begin to lengthen your exhales until they are twice as long as your inhales.

3. Take a slow, three-second inhale, until your lungs are full. Retain your inhale for a count of three.

4. Release the breath slower, taking six counts to exhale. Retain your exhale for a count of three.

5. If you are anxious, do the best you can to try to slow your breath, and breathe all the way into the low belly. Make sure you're expanding the breath deeper than the upper lungs.

6. Repeat the double down breath for two to five minutes or until you feel more at peace.

Alternate Nostril Breath

This breath is used by ancient yogis and contemporary practition-ers alike to balance the right and left hemispheres of your brain. You will definitely notice a marked feeling of focused clarity even after two minutes. It's an antidote to confusion, fatigue, insomnia, and anxiety.

1. Begin the *ujjayi* breath, using four-second inhales and exhales.

2. Curl the first two fingers of your right hand into your palm.

3. Hold the right thumb next to the right nostril and the ring finger next to your left. This classical hand position, or *mudra*, is thought to increase the benefits of the tech-nique. If you find it difficult, just use your thumb and index finger.

4. Press the right nostril closed and breathe a full exhale/inhale through the left nostril only.

5. Then switch sides, pressing the left nostril closed and breathing an inhale/exhale through the right nostril.

6. Continue switching sides after each round of breath for two minutes. Release the nose after you finish with the last inhale on the right side.

7. Finish with a one-minute round of *ujjayi* breathing through both nostrils.

Whenever you're feeling drained, off center, frazzled, or foggy, return to a healing breath. Two minutes of your time spent in rhythmic, intentionalized breathing can not only change the moment at hand, but influence the rest of your day.

Soul Service

Another excellent way to infuse your life with more energetic miles per gallon is to get out there and learn about something that interests you. Whether you want to make money doing something you love but don't know how to do that yet, or you need a new hobby, you can take steps to make it happen!

There are classes, workshops, retreats, and training for any budget. Your local art gallery, university, community center, or YMCA all abound with opportunities. Even if you don't know if you want to become a photographer, or whether you're even any good at it, you can still sign up for a beginner's photography course to find out.

What is it you've been yearning to do? Make pottery on the wheel? Learn yoga? Become a Pilates instructor? Paint? Write? Play guitar like a rock star? Whatever interests you is a direct shot of soul fuel. Find it and learn it, then do more of it.

If you do end up with (or already have) a skill set that you would enjoy sharing, volunteer to teach at your local community center. You'll be working maybe an hour or two a week in a low-pressure environment, giving to people who really want to learn what you know. So in this transaction, everyone wins. By offering what you love to others, you'll fire them up and be warmed by their glow at the same time.

If I had to talk about accounting for five minutes, it would exhaust me. Yet one of my most rewarding times is when I teach students or speak to audiences about the road trip. For hours I discuss and still remain connected to the universal flow, because I'm being passionately of service while doing one of the things I'm meant for.

If you don't feel you have mastered your hobby or field yet, how about teaching kids? You'll learn as they do and probably have some serious fun to boot.

Finding Your Gas Stations

Every day, you come upon and then miss opportunities to enhance your life. Many would take only a few seconds to experience, yet you may either not see them or decide not to take advantage of them in the moment. Responsibilities such as getting to work on time, making an appointment, catching the bus, or getting your errands done can keep your focus moving away from the magic that surrounds you. Remind yourself to look for the soul's gas stations, and they will start to appear.

Filling up isn't something that you do all in one shot and that's it for life. Soul fueling is a daily practice and a process of gathering in. Even little moments, such as my five-minute detour to watch the New Mexican sunrise, pay off big-time as lifelong memories that give me bursts of happiness whenever I think about them. You may not have an hour every day to stop and smell the roses. But I bet you can pause for ten seconds and take one deep breath.

The first step toward recognizing gas stations, these potential sources of energy input, throughout your day is to keep your eyes open. If you pay attention to all the little and big chances you get to infuse your present experience with a little more joie de vivre, you may be amazed at how many crop up along your path.

Nothing exists for you until you bring your awareness to it. It's not that nothing's there before you see it; on the contrary, everything's there. It's like looking for one particular blue-and-white-jacketed book on a shelf, then finding it. You didn't really see the brown and red books. When you choose to focus on one thing, it becomes more prominent in your world. The rest fades into the background.

So choose what types of experiences you want to bring forward. Are you looking up on that city bus to catch the sunset—or are you just mad because it's late? Did you miss the bouquet of flowers at the grocery store that was just waiting for you to get them for yourself—and maybe give a bloom or two to your stressed-out coworkers? If so, don't worry—life is hectic, and sometimes we all hurry through life-enhancing moments. But the more you look for them, the more they will show up for you.

To give you an idea of quick gas station stops you can make instead of their less-energetic counterparts, check out the following list.

If you are running out your tank by:

- Taking a quick mindless shower
- Listening to chaotic street chatter
- Standing in line at the store
- Going to the mall in your baggy sweatpants because who cares?

Then fill 'er up by:

- Taking a five-minute bath (don't forget the bubbles!)
- Getting a music player and filling it with your favorite music or audiobook to listen to during your walks outside or whatever activity makes you feel full of life and learning instead of full of noise.
- Paying the woman in front of you at the check-out line a compliment about her dress, then reaping the benefits of her thank-you and smile.
- Dressing way up—hair, clothes, shoes, everything. You will put more spark in your swish—no matter where you go.

Now create some of your own gas station stops. It takes a bit of extra force to veer off your scheduled path and take the one less traveled. But hey, it's worth it.

A Soul Surround

The final teaching of the gas station will keep you humming with good vibrations all day long. You can set up your environment to consistently infuse you with positive energy, so that no matter where you are, you're immersed in goodness.

What gives you fuel are the things that make you happy, that you're passionate about, and, basically, that make you grin. They are individual to you, and depending on your tastes, you'll create some soul surrounds that will work for you. You might:

- Make a CD of soul songs. They can be anything you wish; just include all the music that inspires, soothes, energizes, or helps you get in touch with your powerful nature. Make different mixes for your various moods.

- Create a journal into which you write quotes and thoughts, paste articles, have pictures, and add anything else that inspires you. Read it often.

- Have something beautiful to look at wherever you are. Buy flowers for your desk at work, get a coffee mug you love, tape up a child's drawing. Ignite the soul any way you can.

- Spend time with children or animals. Whether taking kids on a nature walk or walking a dog, you'll get a reminder that no matter how big your problems seem, there is still the possibility for laughter.

- Carry a special stone, a crystal, or a memento in your pocket. Find something meaningful to you and keep it close. Whenever you touch it, think of something or some-one that makes your heart feel good.

- Mix a cocktail—a bubble-bath cocktail, that is. Go to your local bed and bath store and make a bath infusion of a few ingredients you love. My favorite combination is lavender bath salts, a tablespoon of sweet almond oil, and a little fresh grated orange peel (put the gratings in a metal tea infuser so they don't get everywhere). Soak and enjoy.

Road Rule

Never exit a bathtub or a shower without taking advantage of the acoustics and belting out your favorite song.

This list could be endless. Spend a moment now brainstorming some things you can do to add more shine to your life. As you leave the gas station, keep in mind that staying on full is a discipline of consistency. No matter what your challenges are, find ways to return to the station each day, and you will give yourself the greatest gift of all: the gift of a life you love.

adjust your mirrors

How to Get Positively Self-Centered

my trip
The Day I Stopped Being So Selfless

Not to complain, but it's a fact: I'd just worked forty-seven days straight, to be work-worry free during my two-week vacation, which, now that I'm writing it down, looks imbalanced. But the Big Apple doesn't take kindly to slackers.

By the time I left New York City to see my family in Kansas City, I was 100 percent city-fried. My job as a yoga teacher, speaker, and life coach consisted mostly of taking care of business—mine, and anyone else's who needed me. After all, a spiritual guide is deep in the service of others, and believe me, I served till there was nothing left but crumbs.

If I were my own life coach, I would have benched me. So there I was, finally, on my vacation, helping my old college friend

Christine watch her four kids while her husband, Nick, fixed the roof. I saw him two times in the four days I was there, both after climbing a ladder and handing him the screwdriver "with the cross on the end."

At night, I volunteered to babysit the kids, because Chris and Nick rarely get to go out by themselves, and I care about them enough to sacrifice my quality time with my friends (and my sanity) to let them have a couple of worry-free dates. I love their kids, but babysitting four people under the age of seven when you're exhausted is not fun for anyone. I mean, having kids prepares you, by slowly upping your tolerance. Jumping into a ready-made bunch is not easy. Grilled cheese sandwiches were made. Barney videos came on. The purple monster sang repetitively. My brain slowly went numb.

On the last day, I was packing the few shirts that had managed to survive the visit stain-free and I realized: I'm not in college anymore. None of us are. And now I was about to head to Colorado to stay another five days with Sarah and Dave—two friends who have three kids, two dogs, and a ferret named Rocky, and who run a day care center inside their home.

It's not that I didn't want to see Sarah. I did. It was just that, in my already depleted state, I knew I really didn't *need* to see her. To force myself to continue on to Colorado would be the last drop gone from my already emptying tank.

As I was driving away from Chris's house, I decided that what would be best for *me* was to make the space and time to reconnect with myself, by doing what people do on vacations—*relax*. My whole being just needed a break—before I had a breakdown.

I pulled into a Wal-Mart parking lot and called Sarah. She was understandably very disappointed, and so was I. But I knew I was out. Done, kaput—no more mojo in my dojo. I had nothing of quality left to give the relationship at that time, and I knew having to show up for people in that state would deplete me even more. I decided, for the first time in a long while, to stop draining away my life energy for others, no matter who the others were. True friends would never want that to happen. And so I spoke honestly, no excuses, and told her that I would have to see her on another trip. It was hard to hear her disappointment without taking it personally or wanting to go back on my decision.

After I got off the phone, I sat in the parking lot. It was just seven in the morning and quiet—the few other cars parked over in the corner belonged to the employees. I could be alone and deal with my decision, which, for someone who loves nothing more than pleasing other people, was a very hard one. I breathed deeply, and breathed some more, through the waves of immense guilt that I was leaving my friend in the lurch, that I was a terrible person, and that what little energy I had belonged to everyone else except for me. I felt selfish for hanging on to it.

Then the "shoulds" came up: that I should have gone, that I should have some integrity and keep my word—even though the only thing I wanted to do was sleep for two straight days. What kind of person could choose a nap over her best friend? How dare I! This went on for an hour before I could breathe easier. Finally, in the middle of an inhale, my inner teacher stepped forward and said, "Hey, wait a minute! Sometimes you have to temporarily disappoint people in order to take care of yourself. If they really love you, they will choose you to be happy over having to see you. Besides, if you know this is best for you, and you believe that what's best for you is ultimately best for everyone, then what are you worried about right now? Get moving! You have a vacation to enjoy!" I turned the key in the ignition. Then I backed out and turned the car around slowly, not sure where to go next.

I now had five days all to myself. I couldn't remember the last time that had happened. No boyfriend here, no friends, and no family relying on my love and support. No job responsibilities. Not even a plant to water or someone else's baby to coo at. I was only thirty years old and already life weighed heavily on me. Healers are often like Atlas, trying to hold up the world—theirs and other people's. So I decided right then and there to lighten up.

I drove the car in a slow circle, and when my foot decided to hit the accelerator, I took off in a new, surprise direction. Where I would end up, I couldn't say, but at the end of my wonderful, me-time adventures in Memphis, Tennessee, after five days of sleep, good food, soaking in my hotel's hot tub, and writing about all of it in my journal over excellent coffee, I was really glad I'd gotten up the nerve to adjust my perspective to become positively self-centered.

And Sarah? She decided to use her five days with no house-guest to finally mail the poetry she'd been writing but never had the courage to submit for publication. I'd made her mad enough to do it. She was published, and continues to be, one of her biggest dreams come true.

At the time, Sarah was miffed that I canceled our plans. But since it was best for me, I had to rely on the belief that it was somehow best for her, too. I hoped she'd thank me later, and later, she did.

the map
Reset Your Mirrors

This stop will help you adjust your mirrors to keep perspective on the ways you see yourself and your world, as well as how those around you perceive you. Shifting your perspectives will make your life reflect your strengths rather than your weaknesses.

How can you become more understanding of what you need, pay enough attention to yourself, and make moves to benefit you without becoming negatively narcissistic?

The answers are found here, and to discover them you must learn about a very important spiritual practice—one that is unnecessarily controversial but, when done properly, can change your life forever. It is the practice of becoming more self-centered.

Being self-centered has gotten a negative reputation within some circles. The misunderstanding arose when people confused it with selfishness. Every emotion or state of being has a positive and a negative polarity, the ability to become either destructive or constructive. Self-centering uses the same energy as selfishness, only it's a higher form of it, and therefore it can be healing instead of hurtful. Spiritual disciplines such as yoga are built around this concept of moving into and from your center. Yet the word has taken on a negative cast. I want you now to reclaim its deeper meaning: consider the point of your road trip to be finding ways to give *at least* as much validity and respect to yourself as you give to others. In time, you'll come to see yourself as the ultimate authority on what you need.

The opposite of being self-centered, selflessness, has come to be the ultimate goal of many a seeker. Most aware human beings are compelled to offer themselves to help others. Being selfless is one way to do that, to help ease the world's suffering, by reaching out and supporting your fellow man. It's beautiful, and crucial to our survival. But it's also only one aspect of us that, without its complement, will crumble under its own weight, and disappear. That's because you cannot *only* give out—without giving out.

Self-centering helps you achieve balance. Just as we require the dark to be able to see a candle's flame or need questions to know our answers, we also must engage in a regular practice of drawing into the core of our being to allow us to be able to give more effectively, and without a negative energy drain. Selfless offering is made possible only through a deep connection with your self.

In yoga, the highest form of self-centering is known as *satya*, or truth. I'm not referring to opinion, which many people mistake for truth. In Eastern philosophy, we say that aligning with love is the only truth that ignites real freedom. When we think, speak, and act from this place, we can never be led astray. We develop an ability to see in the dark, to navigate the unknown moments of life while using the sense of higher knowing we all possess.

In many spiritual disciplines, drawing into darkness symbolizes movement inside: introspection, prayer, the journey within, and forging a meaningful relationship with our soul. Light symbolizes our offerings, actions that move who you are out into the world.

When you pause to check your mirrors, you'll learn to move inside before all else and reflect your wisdom back into your daily interactions through aligned actions and words. This practice will make everything you give more true to your heart.

Learning to journey inside and come out stronger and more knowledgeable is to become a more powerful creator. The more you release all truths except those of love and respect for yourself and your fellow man and see yourself as the source of all things, the more effective you will be at whatever you choose to become.

Mirror the Sun

You probably think the sun is a great example of selflessness. After all, it generates and gives light and warmth to millions. But, in fact, it is able to exist and give us life because of its inner core, which is unfathomably dense. The sun's center is drawing in so strongly that its gravitational pull holds all the other planets in orbit. I'd like you to emulate this example.

If the sun's core suddenly disappeared, all its radiance would also vanish. Not only that, but the life forms and planets it supports would cease to exist.

Following nature's example, you can cultivate daily practices that reconnect and draw you into your innermost places and the source that feeds their power. We'll call it "making a core connection." If you don't cultivate this connection, you are much more likely to begin fading in life force and spin wildly off your axis, dimming yourself and affecting everyone around you.

Maintaining your core connection is the key to continually creating your life as you want it to be, while giving to others and without giving yourself away in the process—burning bright without burning out.

Many spiritual students have one or more gurus whom they love to be around. The best gurus are people who know that anyone can become as powerful as they are. I take issue with the person who tells you he or she has something spiritual that you don't, because I know that you have the capacity to be as wise and magnetic as any guru. So if you run across a teacher who says he or she is the only one who can be that powerful, run the other way, fast.

The word *guru* can mean "dense or heavy one." True masters, like the sun, have spent so much time drawing inward that they develop a strong gravitational pull, and people begin to orbit around them. They have drawn in so much that they have attained a continual and conscious link to the universal source. True masters, and they can be anyone, shine from their core, and others gather to bask in their glow. These gurus seem to radiate life energy and are known to balance and heal others just by being in their presence.

There's no reason you can't attain a similar state of being. Let's find out how.

Change Your Worldview

People are generally better at giving than receiving. But if you want to be like the sun, you must get more comfortable with accepting energetic gifts as well as handing them out. This infusion of love travels through you to your soul's core whenever you fully accept the good things that come into your life. Then, like tending a plant, you must keep it alive and growing by nurturing it at the roots.

Balance your selflessness with self-centering and aim to do both *fully* and at the same time, so you are rarely depleted but instead are radiating love in both directions: inside and out. Through adjusting your mirrors to catch the light, you'll begin to locate your awareness back into your center and then balance this action by offering an intelligent amount of your energy back into your relationships and the larger world community.

It can make many givers uncomfortable to hold back and to think a little more about their own happiness, especially when what is in their best interests does not meet another's expectations. That's understandable. No one likes to say "I can't give right now," yet doing exactly that can sometimes be the best thing for everyone. It's uncomfortable and challenging, yet it is the only way to experience your true power and allow others the gift of experiencing theirs.

It may seem, as you go through the practices in this chapter, that you are not caring about others enough. Rest assured that what I am teaching you in this stop will apply to and benefit everyone else you know. You'll get to enrich your relationships at future stops. But to do that, it's crucial that you learn exactly how to turn inward, to listen, and to recognize what is best for you in each situation, *before all else.*

The payoff of this practice is that you will be able to give more completely of your heart and soul. Trust that your relationships *will* benefit from your self-centering discipline, because when you emerge, it will be to offer your heart at a level you might never have before.

Road Rule

What is best for you
in any given situation is
best for all parties involved.

It may not seem like it at the time, but when you do something that's necessary for your spiritual growth, it gives permission to those around you to grow in the way *they* most need. If they are not able to thrive at your new level, then you gave them the gift of freedom to be exactly where they need to be, and you're free to do the same. In the end, be loving, be brave, and be where you are most happy. Whatever the outcome, you just gave the best gift of all: remaining true to your truth.

Your Solar System

In your new worldview, *you* are at the center of your own universe yet, in a healthy, balanced interaction, you are also a planet orbiting in other people's universes, only *they* are at the center of theirs. All of these elements interact as we simultaneously make our individual core connections and share our lives in loving intersection.

It is in this way that we can each take responsibility for our own selves even as we relate to others. This powerful shift, when practiced by even one person in a relationship, will produce immense results toward the good of both. When practiced by both people? Brilliant.

Who's on First?

You're on first. You are always on first. You always will be on first.

You are on first base, the ground floor, the foundation of every decision, every action, every thought you have or words you decide to speak. For this reason, when you readjust your mirrors to make things better, you must look to yourself first.

When dealing with anyone about anything that requires an agreement or action, you'll now pause and check in with yourself before replying. If you worry about what others want or need before you know what *you* need, you will begin to diffuse your core, and everyone will suffer the consequences. It's exactly like losing the sun's life-sustaining power.

The experience of letting someone else's needs override your own is commonly known as "losing oneself," as in, "Wow, I really lost myself in that relationship." Usually it takes a period of being single, and a whole lot of time with good friends, to get yourself back.

The goal is to never give yourself away to the point that you lose a strong bond with your core connection. There's a difference between taking someone's needs into consideration and letting another person run your life. A key point to remember is that your soul never actually goes anywhere. It just *is*, and always will be, right there with you. You can never really lose it, but the less time you spend in relationship with it, the more effort it takes to reestablish consistent contact. So it's easy to feel as if you've lost yourself while in a dysfunctional relationship, because your inner strength appears to be gone, and you can't seem to find it. Think of your soul as a crystal ball. If it's covered in dust, you won't be able to see into it easily, and your answers could get murky.

Let's pause here for a very important question, one I'm often asked: How do you contact your soul?

Connecting to the center of your being is much like using a Magic-8 Ball, the toy that reveals an answer when you shake it up. Do the Inner Teacher technique from your map until you receive an answer. Is the answer unclear? Ask again until you get one that feels right.

If your goal is to be balanced, rooted in your own strength and more capable in your decision making and relationships, and you are asking the universe to bring more of that state to you, then you will want to make healthy self-centering part of your personality.

I'm not asking you to become egomaniacal or to ignore everyone else's needs. But neither is it spiritual to listen compassionately to other people's requests and then give them whatever they want, regardless of your own happiness. If everyone enabled everyone else to realize his or her own inner potential, instead of enabling dysfunction, the world would be a much different place.

Road Rule

If someone could do something themselves, and should do it themselves, then by all means, let them do it themselves.

So from now on, at the foundation of every intention, choice, and action, think of yourself first. I invite you to sit without speaking until you get through your urge to make another person feel better. I want you to go deeper still, through any reactions, dysfunctions, and fears. Deeper until you begin to feel calm, strong, and loving, and clear about what you need. This process may not be a fast one, depending on the situation. But take as much time as you must to figure out what you need to feel balanced and well met in the relationship. Then come back into the situation, and ask for it. If offering help is needed, and you have it to give, then give it. But now you will know if you are able to or not.

Replacing "Should"

People often use the word *should* when they don't really want to do something but feel that they have to. The dictionary states that one main function of *should* in modern American English is to "express duty, obligation, etc."

This week, pay attention to how you use the word (and what you really mean by it): "I should go to her birthday party (although I don't really appreciate how she treats me)," "I should stay on the phone (draining myself listening to this drama because he really seems to need my advice)," and so forth.

"Should" can represent powerlessness as does its counterpart "can't." When you use one of these words, see if it is a cue that someone else's needs are overriding your own. What you're really saying is, "I don't want to, but I'm going to anyway," or "I'm not strong enough to be able to do that." Using this language means you've given your power over to that person for the moment, no matter how small, and those little moments add up.

When it comes to you speaking about your choices and actions, I encourage you to start using the words *will* and *won't* in place of *should* or *can't*. Those two small words, *will* and *won't*, make you the master of your own moment and instantly empower you. The word *will*, meaning "to agree to do something," has a few additional meanings:

- The faculty of conscious and especially of deliberate action; the power of control the mind has over its own actions; the freedom of the will

- The power of choosing one's own actions

- The act or process of using or asserting one's choice; volition

I don't know about you, but this is much more my style than the word *obligation*. There are two responses to any situation or request. Either you *choose* to do something for yourself or another person—or you choose not to. Make the decision that feels best for you and the state of your time and energy, and then say, "I will do this" or "I won't." If you decide to do something, own it, then undertake it with integrity. If you choose not to, hold your ground.

Even if you are undergoing something intense that was brought upon you by another's choice, you can still decide if you will or won't allow it to drain your life force. This is why one of our strongest inner energies is called *willpower*. Reclaiming your power of choice is one of the fastest ways to hop back into the driver's seat.

Tilt Your Mirrors away from Guilt

If you truly believed that your highest actions were for the greatest good of those you love, you'd probably take those actions with a clear conscience, yes? Yet there is an incredible amount of guilt and mistrust of one's own wisdom when confronted with actually doing that. Why is it so hard to say no to people, or to say, "I have to leave this relationship" or "I would be happier doing something else"? To get to what's best for others, you must first do what's best for you. And especially if what will make you happiest isn't what other people think they want, they may not yet see that their greater good is being served and may react badly. This disparity can be so painful that it seems easier to just say yes and stay where you are not in alignment, to ease the discomfort of those you care about.

To self-center in the face of difficulty, you must be willing to stand firm while those around you scowl, blame, cry, and react. They may not do this, but be prepared for it: many people resist change, few people like feeling second place to your needs, and even fewer like to be told no, no matter how lovingly. But on the road trip, every conscious no is ultimately a yes to the soul. If you really love someone, love him or her enough to reveal who you really are, and let this person have all the information, not just selected parts.

I had a friend who wanted to share an apartment with me. She came to me with the idea, all excited. I, however, knew that our lifestyles were incompatible, since she had a cat and liked to get up early, and I'm allergic to cats and like to stay up late. Apartments aren't big in the Big Apple, not big enough to mask the clanking of breakfast dishes two hours before my alarm goes off. So I told her that, although I cherished her friendship, I would pass on the roommate situation. She didn't speak to me for a few weeks, because she was hurt by my answer. Then the perfect one-bedroom apartment presented itself to her, and she called to thank me before the ink was dry on her (rent-stabilized) lease.

When you muster up the courage to share what you've learned at your self's center, all the people concerned enter into the moment with a clear idea of what they are agreeing to. If they can compromise with you, then you will get what you want and so will they. If they can't, they won't. But at least you were honest. Maybe this exchange is a one-time interaction that isn't a big deal, or maybe it's a whole relationship you must say "I will" or "I won't" to. Self-centering is useful at all points of the spectrum.

Resistance to fully standing up and being yourself, especially in the important moments, is really the fear of being alone. Within that are the fears of not being accepted, that you don't really know what you need, that you'll never find another man, woman, job, friend, and so on. You still must trust the light of your initial intuition. If you make your decisions from a fear-based place, you can be sure that they will not be constructive for any of your relationships.

If you do choose to give something inauthentic in the moment, to avoid pain, disappointment, or loss, you might gain the immediate satisfaction of having someone or something remain near to you, but you will lose touch with your soul, remaining blocked from giving or

Road Rule

Turn all mirrors to face the road of your soul's grandest dreams. Then you'll always see the right way to go.

receiving completely. So let's move on and take actions that will clear the way to your deepest truth.

take the wheel
Speak with Integrity

From now on, when answering a question or offering any verbal comment, take the road of highest integrity: say what you feel is the best representation of your truth, and only that.

I'm not asking you to tell Aunt Millie once and for all that her muumuu dress looks like a curtain. Speaking with integrity doesn't mean that you say things with disrespect or blurt out any thought that comes up. You must keep your compassion filter in place.

Rather, this is a daily discipline of staying in constant inner contact, so when there's something you want to express and you've waited until you feel clearly aligned with your deepest needs, you'll be able to say it out loud in a way that is in harmony with who you are. Think of it as tuning your words to a high frequency, as much as you are using your intentions and emotions. Whenever you speak, you are saying it right to the universe's face. So say it with honor.

This approach also applies to the words with which you leak energy during mundane conversations. If a discussion is not meaningful to you, don't participate in it. Even spending time listening to someone else who is boring or irritating you is a form of energy drain. You know when you feel enlivened or weakened by talking or listening to others talk. Find your way out of an unpleasant conversation gracefully, and get back to your trip, pronto.

To find the words that will best serve your desire to retain and express your core connection, follow these steps:

1. Close your lips. If you physically can't talk, you won't. Get quiet, and pause your speech. If you're around other people, use some of the most powerful words ever invented: "Excuse me."

2. Contact your Inner Teacher. Wait until you know what you need to say (if anything) from a place of inner strength and

self-respect. If each of your words cost you five dollars, which ones would you spend on this moment?

3. Mirror your words. How would you feel if someone spoke to you using the words you've chosen? It doesn't matter if you're responding to a heated situation or an innocuous one; act with dignity.

4. Say it. Speak your mind (and heart and soul). Keep it short and sweet. Even expressing your truth for too long becomes draining. Stand in support of yourself and know that whatever you say, when you truly mean it, once is enough.

5. Let it echo. Let there be silence now. Most people try to jump in and fill the space before and after a clear statement, which blocks the process of receiving. Allow the discomfort of silence after you speak. Let the other person hear the echo of what you said and take it to heart if he or she chooses. You will also gather in the energetic ripples of your words by pausing to do so after you've said something powerful.

Mirror In, Mirror Out

To become more positively self-centered, you must know where—and how—to look. It's no wonder getting to know your soul is called a time of reflection. Like so many things of a spiritual nature, reflections happen in two ways: internally, between you and yourself, and externally, between you and other people. Whatever angle you look from in your own mirror as well as the ones that others hold up to you can cause your core connection to either strengthen or weaken. If you learn how to see yourself properly, you will become expert at using these two types of mirrors to your advantage.

People hold mirrors up to you all the time. They do this through their comments, opinions, and statements about who you are—to them. These mirrors are yours to keep or to break. No one can know you as well as you know yourself, so take every outside reflection into account, but now add a hefty dose of skepticism.

Use the suggestions in the following sections to receive the positive reflections of yourself. The negative ones? If you get enough of them, maybe take a look at your choices. Move into closer alignment with good vibrations, then choose to gaze into more positive mirrors instead. They each help you reflect upon the greatness inside you.

Learn to Take a Compliment

Compliments come in many forms: a nice comment, a kind gesture, help and loving support. So often, we squirm in discomfort whenever someone says or does something really nice, especially if it's directed right at us. "Oh, stop!" we say, when we would benefit more from saying "Oh, go on!" Why is that?

Wholeheartedly accepting a compliment, or any positive mirroring, requires that you realize that you're pretty awesome. Too many times, we agree with more negative assessments of our character, and we resist the good ones.

Whenever you deflect a heartfelt compliment, it's like slamming a door on the person who gave it. That individual is offering you a gift. Don't throw it away; rip off the paper, open it, really take it in, smile big, and simply say, "Thank you."

Give It to Yourself

The process of self-centering you are embarking upon includes the practice of believing that you are as worthy of being cherished as much as anyone else on this earth. In the end, nobody can ever mirror you well enough to make you believe this. You cannot get enough reassurance or love from another person to make you positive that you're okay. You must take the wheel of your own destiny and deliberately choose to allow yourself to be as extraordinary as you really are. Every day, give yourself compliments. Write an e-mail to yourself letting you know how much you appreciate all the work you've done and all the attention you're giving toward you. While you're at it, compliment others, even those you feel jealous of or irritated by. By going out of your way to say something nice, something you really feel, you will recharge the part of you that flows through love instead of through competition or judgment.

Throw a Mirror Party

Gather together one or more people you trust. It can be anything from a casual kitchen meeting with your husband or wife to a soiree complete with cocktails and finger food. The point of this gathering is to practice fully receiving positive mirrors from other people.

Here's how you do it. Begin by sitting together in a quiet place. Have the other person give you a major compliment. Not "Hey, those jeans make you look like you lost ten pounds," which is very nice but not world-shaking. Let someone tell you what you mean to him or her and share the qualities this person recognizes and values in you. Look into the eyes of the individual who is offering this gift to you. Pay attention to the reactions you experience while being given this compliment. Is your breathing slow and even? Are you embarrassed, nervous, or uncomfortable? If so, welcome to the club. Keep breathing and take a moment of silence after the statement and close your eyes.

Let the intentions behind the compliment—the love—sink deeper, through layers of resistance, doubt, fear, and insecurity, until you feel it drop into the vast inner ocean of your soul. You will sense a peace come upon you, and a quiet strength. Your heart may begin to expand and lighten, and at this point, open your eyes, look at your partner, and simply say, "Thank you." At this point, you should mean it. Resist saying anything more or complimenting the person right back, as this can be another way to deflect receiving. Go into another room alone for at least five more minutes and allow the niceness to really sink in completely. Then, if you want, switch sides and show someone a positive mirror of your own.

Flip the Mirror

We hold up mirrors to ourselves and one another all the time and either accept or deny what we see based on our beliefs about who we are.

What you believe creates your reality. Yet beliefs are changeable. Therefore, if part of your creation isn't working to bring out the best in you, you might consider switching those diminishing beliefs for something that does. I call this practice *flipping the mirror*.

Say someone held up a double-sided mirror to you, and it made you look distorted, ugly, and ashamed of what you saw. But if you turned it around, you looked radiant, beautiful, and loved what you saw. Which side would you rather choose?

People hand you both constructive and destructive mirrors all day long. Those mirrors are solely based on *their* truths, which in turn are based on their individual opinions. What one person loves about you the next person may find completely irritating, and vice versa—opinions are relative. Who are you going to listen to? As the final authority, listen to yourself.

Surround yourself with people who mirror you positively and who support you to use your talents. Great friends call you out on your issues, but they do it rarely and from a place of caring and with compassion. Critical people hold the most destructive mirrors of all. The next time someone, even your own inner critic, reflects you in a weakening way, mentally picture flipping that mirror over. Find a way to reflect the situation to yourself in a more empowering way, because, no matter what's going on, there always is one. If someone hands you too many negative mirrors, downgrade that person's presence in your life. You should not have to constantly flip mirrors away from one person. The inner critic is enough to handle.

Use this example: In your mind's destructive mirror, you see yourself as overweight and out of control. Flip this mirror, and say. "Wow! All that food I've been eating tasted so good! Now, I'm going to eat better and exercise more, starting with a fifteen-minute walk today. I'll get back in the shape of my life. Until then, I'm still going to wear that red dress tonight!"

You don't have to bring yourself down or continue to let anyone else make you feel smaller just to observe something you want to change, when there are a million more loving perspectives available. Spend the moments of your precious life to change what you can, accept the rest, and enjoy being alive. In the final analysis, we will not remember the petty dramas of life—only the quality of our days, so let's not regret a single second, starting now.

Breaking Mirrors

I once had a boyfriend who couldn't stand the way I flossed my teeth; my current partner happily flosses away right next to me. Truth is relative to each individual, and with billions of truths out there, are you going to balance your self-worth on such an unstable principle? Your truth is the ultimate one for you, as others' are to them—and it's up to you to shatter these destructive mirrors by shifting your beliefs wherever and whenever you choose. You do this by simply looking away from mean mirrors and the mean or unconscious people that hold them up to you. Only invite others into your intimate circle who more properly reflect your inner worth. To break a destructive, negative belief, realize that you are greater than any one mirror. Ignore the comment, refuse to participate, remove yourself from the dynamic, set boundaries, and choose to make more space for the positive. There is a difference between constructive and destructive criticism. Even in the midst of wanting to upgrade, you can take any shadow aspect of yourself, hold it up to the mirror, and say in strength and love: "This is a part of me—and I'm working on it." Anything less should be broken and walked away from forever. Sense the glass crunching under your feet as you leave the scene of a shattered hurtful mirror. It's the best feeling ever.

Make a Magic Mirror

Go out today and pick up some markers that wipe off of glass easily. Then pick a mirror in your house to decorate. The bathroom mirror is good because you're in there a lot, stopping at it to thoroughly brush and floss your teeth. Around the border of this mirror, I want you to write things like, "You're human. But you're also divine" or "You rock. Nothing can change that fact but you." Write inspiring quotes there, love letters to yourself, something great someone said about you—whatever gets you in a good mood and reminds you to stay there.

If it's a family mirror, even better—have everyone offer kudos to one another, and whoever looks into it will be getting messages sent straight from the heart.

The magic mirror will continue to remind you about your natural state of excellence whenever you're in doubt.

Superpowers, Activate!

Clark Kent's alter ego is Superman; Peter Parker's is Spiderman. Now you get to create an alter ego that is as heroic as you can imagine.

As though emerging from a phone booth while ripping off your suit and tie, this alter ego will include all the most amazing aspects of yourself from which you can draw strength and act in ways that show everyone else how super you really are.

Road Rule

In each moment,
be-have: *be* now what
you wish to *have* later.
Do you want love? *Be* love.

This practice gets you to choose, out of everything you could be, who and what you *will* be.

Choosing your superhero self might sound like a child's game, but, in fact, it gives you the power to choose and *behave* as that greatness above anything else. Then, every day, you will reveal to other people the brightest and most heroic in you, without trying to dim or hide your brilliance. Why should you diminish yourself?

First, make a list of all your superhero qualities. If you need suggestions, rent any of the Marvel Comics movies, or consider aspects of people who inspire you.

Qualities of the hero include:

- Determination
- Strength of character
- Fighting for justice
- Living with integrity
- Compassion in the face of suffering

Notice as you write that there is nothing on your list that you don't already possess.

My best friend, Milly, is a wonderful example of how and why to create an alter ego. She said, "I used to be someone who was extremely vulnerable and swayed by other people's opinions of me. I went from relationship to relationship hanging on my partner's every word. If he said he loved me one day, I felt great. If he was in a bad mood, or criticized me, I felt awful.

"I never believed I had it in me to stand up and be a strong person, especially when I was in love. It got so bad that I didn't think I could live if one particular man left me. When he eventually did, I seriously contemplated ending everything. Not because I thought I deserved it, but because I'd given him so much importance, that I believed that since he was gone, so was my future.

"Something that helped me immensely was to create an alter ego I call Diamond Girl. When I was weak, Diamond Girl took over with all the strength I felt I lacked. Of course, it was me doing everything, but it helped to feel that maybe something in me could rescue me for once, instead of me waiting for someone else to save me.

"Diamond Girl would get me out of bed and make me go out, get back to my life's work, and slowly heal from the breakup. She made me order the filet mignon when I felt too depressed to eat.

And she even made me brave enough to ask my friends and family for support if I needed it.

"In the end, she became me—because she *was* me all along. Now I am so much more capable in my relationships with everyone, and much less swayed from my center.

"Knowing that Diamond Girl is always there to have my back if I need her has changed me for the better. Who knew little old me had a superhero inside?"

Now, just like Diamond Girl, you'll need a superhero name. This is a fun thing to brainstorm with friends. To find the name, you must discern what your most unique superpower is. It can be a heart quality or something you're excellent at doing. You have one superpower above all others that's special to you. You might call this your gift. If you're not sure, think about how and when you've been able to help people. What do your closest relationships say your supertalent is? Do you love well? Listen well? Make cranberry-almond scones well? Are you thoughtful and always have a lawn mower at the ready in case your neighbor's is on the fritz again? Everyone has a superhero inside. What's yours?

Keep your alter ego name somewhere close, such as in your wallet, or draw a picture of him or her and tack it to your refrigerator. Now whenever you're seeking the path toward your soul, and your center seems very far away, you have a superhero who will come to your rescue. You'll always turn toward yourself first and then bravely deal with whatever comes your way by activating your best qualities. You have all of this power available to you at every moment.

As you leave this stop, remember to take with you the ability to pause, make a core connection, mirror yourself in constructive ways, and then choose to take the actions of your biggest hero, *you*. The strength you gain from becoming a reflection of your highest truth on the inside and out will be immense.

the weighing station

Drop What's Weighing You Down—and Lighten Up!

my trip
When I Finally Learned to Let Go

I was leaving Los Angeles in the morning on a road trip forced by the breakdown of my two-year relationship. I was leaving one of my soul mates, whom I'd met either too soon or too late. I never did decide which one it was. My boyfriend and I had resisted and fought it (along with each other), but in the end we'd come to the conclusion that our soul mate–ness was not enough to stop our humanity from getting in the way. To make matters worse, all of my suitcases were missing.

At the time, all I wanted, besides my partner back, was to own and run an art gallery. I'd gotten the opportunity to return to Iowa and do just that. It was a creative and exciting offer, and one that was perfect in its timing, as I would come to understand years later.

"One out of two ain't bad," I tried to assure myself, bolstering my heart as I prepared to go through all the things my boyfriend and I had collected together, as well as my own belongings. It was almost ten o'clock at night, and I still hadn't taken my clothes out of our closet or separated my records from his. By midnight, I'd made a big pile in the center of the apartment, and paused to ask the universe to give me a sign: should I just set it on fire in effigy? Luckily, no sign appeared, yet there were so many memories of us in that pile, I wasn't sure if I could handle having them around. Even that stupid chipped yellow coffee cup was a reminder of so many mornings spent laughing and talking about a future together that would never happen.

Reason won out, and I began searching for my suitcases. Time would heal everything, and I would be able to look at my belongings objectively again, someday. I had extremely large suitcases, and I was going to need them, since it seemed I'd kept every little trinket I'd ever accumulated in my life—half-used tubes of ancient lipstick, old movie ticket stubs, birthday cards from people I didn't even remember.

I looked everywhere, but my luggage had vanished. It was deeply puzzling—I'd used it just a month before. But, as I would be leaving in the morning, I had to think fast. I got five extra-thick trash bags, sat in front of my huge pile of stuff, and began to say the following mantra: "What goes with me, and what can I now let go?"

I sat there silently repeating this for about an hour, as I looked at all the things I'd gathered around me up until then. The night was still and hot, and suddenly, the pile seemed to shimmer as if it were a dip in the highway, turned watery under the fierce noontime sun. Certain items began to stand out from the mirage. They looked brighter than the rest, and I felt compelled to begin plucking them out of the pile like jewels from sand. I thought for sure I was imagining the entire thing, and maybe I was. But after another hour, I'd made two distinct piles—Things to Take, and Things to Trash.

What shocked me the most was realizing that the To Take pile contained almost solely my belongings. The partnership items were going to remain behind, and in that moment I had a flash of freedom—from the pain, the drama, and the struggle of a relationship that held a lot of love but was no longer healthy or meant to be. The reminders of our once-happy time together now held little positive meaning for me. If I would take them, it would be out of the fear of letting go, of letting him go, and of releasing my plan for us that would never be. That whole pile of stuff, just material and energetic baggage now, would be just that much more weight I would carry into the future. My heart was heavy enough as it was. I didn't want to forget the lessons or the love; I never forgot, and I never will. But I wanted to lighten my load, inside and out, so I could move forward, unencumbered.

It didn't feel right to put my good things in garbage bags, so I filled all five with the trash pile, and it fit exactly. I took a black marker and made a sign that said, "These were my things. I loved them. Please find them a good home." Then I took them down to the street and bid them good-bye. I felt freer, somehow. As I walked back up the stairs, I nearly bounced.

As I passed my neighbor's door, something shiny caught my eye. There, under the stairs, were all my suitcases! I'd forgotten I had left them there because there had been no more room for them in the apartment. I packed the keeper pile in two of my three suitcases. I took the third to the street and left it next to the trash bags with another note. This one read: "For you to carry only the most meaningful things you find here—and love—into your future."

When I left in the morning and got out on the open road, I looked into the backseat and saw my two suitcases sitting neatly there. I smiled and felt the possibility of what lay ahead of me and knew I could move on, unpacked from the past.

the map
Just Let Go

If you want to make, and keep, your life the way you want it, you must be willing to let go of what it is you do *not* want. In any major spiritual discipline, the principle of simplicity is seen as a prerequisite of growth. To go forward, you must have made the space to move. We clear this space on three levels: mind (your thoughts), body (your emotions), and action (taken in the world).

No matter who you are, you're sure on some level to find some messes lurking: a life-threatening broom closet, unpaid debts, unsaid "I'm sorry's," insecurity, binge-eating, lack of exercise, self-hatred, anger. Those chaotic places are the true indicators of your state of mind, of heart, and, most important, the level of flow you are currently resisting or allowing.

If you are someone who can't let go of the past; who has inner chaos, stuffed and hidden emotions; or who has trouble dropping any of your physical, mental, or emotional baggage, it will show up in your life as relationship trouble, failed ventures, and a host of other undesirables. I count a hyperorganized, tightly controlled and guarded life to be just as misaligned as a supermessy one. And guess what? Nobody's perfect, and working with our baggage is a lifelong process. Make sure you don't chastise yourself and add more negative weight. Simply shed light upon those places that are so loaded with junk that they're restricting your life from working properly.

If you want to be more effective as a person, a lover, and a friend; be successful and happy; *and* have a strong sense of self from which to create your life as you dreamed it could be, you have to get rid of everything, and I mean *everything*, that is consistently getting in your way.

An important thing to realize about baggage of any kind is that one really messy or crowded area drags you down in every other way and on every other level. There is no separation between that broom closet and your inner self. Whenever you have stuff dumped all over the place, it's like having piles of garbage in your energetic living room: you can't find all of your ground.

Eastern philosophies teach us the art of intentional organization, meditation techniques to clear the mind of extraneous thought, and how to develop true forgiveness for lightening the heart. These practices will give you room to welcome in the things you choose and reclaim the entire ground of your center. Here at the weighing station, you will master each of them so as to shed all your excess baggage and choose only what you wish to take along for the next part of your journey.

In the West, where having a lot of stuff is a status symbol, we are just beginning to understand the value of having less. We're realizing that the benefits of living simply on all levels apply directly to our modern lives: our minds, hearts, and homes have become cluttered with old stories, defenses, self-doubt, meaningless stuff, painful memories, and other heavy things we've been hanging onto for dear life—until now.

You never need to clear the soul or remove clutter from it. The soul is always a Zen garden. But to get to it, we first have to clean the three layers of environment, body, and mind. If any one of them is in a state of disarray, you will not be able to fully experience the rest.

This stop is like a car wash for the soul. After a time of diligent practice, you will look up and realize that from the driver's seat, you can see straight through its windows to the wondrous landscape that is your center. And that, my friend, will be a very good day.

First, let's learn the philosophy behind all three areas.

Outer Space

You don't have to go far to get to outer space. Just sit on your couch or a chair and look around you. Outer space is any area where you spend a lot of your time and have some amount of decision-making power over the environment: your home, your car, your office. If you can decorate it, it's your outer space.

Look around your house, your desk, the inside of your car. Look closely at your bedroom, your bathroom, your dining room, and your kitchen. Most of us have it pretty together on this level because we know other people will see it.

But look deeper, behind closed doors, in such areas as closets, medicine cabinets, desk drawers, and, if you're lucky enough to have any of these things—unlike many of us here in the city who consider room for a flower box a luxury—your garage, basement, and attic. The real measure of your inner state can be found in the state of your hiding places.

You can hide disarray from other people, but you can't hide it from yourself. You know it's there, and you're vibrating at a lower level because of it. Outer areas of chaos signal that something on the inside is not quite aligned with your soul's intentions. That means part of you is in dissonance, and the universe will respond to it.

If you live, drive, and work amid enough disorganization and negative energy vibes, you can experience negative physical and mental effects—such as stress, insomnia, and illness—all from practicing neglect of your outer alignment. Don't think that your soul and the universe don't know what's under your bed—they do. Luckily, every messy outer space is an opportunity. It is another chance for you to realign, right now, with your highest intentions. When you do this, your space resonates more highly, you feel more empowered, and you create a new matrix of energy that can heal, calm, and open you to greater insights. Or you can slow the creative process by being unmindful of your things. Now if that isn't a reason to go through that huge pile of old papers and magazines, I don't know what is!

The Heart

One of my favorite parables goes like this: A monk and his elderly Master were walking to the next town, and they came upon a river with no bridge. When they got to the banks, they realized that the water was shallow enough to walk across and also that there was a man standing there, looking right at them. The man seemed at the peak of health, yet he asked the Master if he could carry him across. "I don't want to get my nice shoes wet," he explained.

So the Master hoisted him upon his back and carried him across, as the monk walked alongside, shaking his head and muttering. At the other side of the river, the Master put the man down and they parted ways without a word of thanks. The monk appeared angry and looked down as he walked, lips tight. Finally, after two hours of this, the Master asked the monk, "Brother, why are you so upset?" The monk unleashed a tirade against the man, saying, "He was so rude! He didn't care if your shoes got wet, as long as his didn't. He didn't care if you were a Master of considerable age—he just hopped right onto your back. He didn't even say 'thank you' when you so nicely put him down! I can't believe his rudeness!" The Master stopped, looked into the monk's eyes, and calmly said, "Brother, I put that man down on the other side of the river and two hours later, you're still carrying him."

Letting go or putting down what you've been lugging around in your heart doesn't mean that you forget about people or lose the memories or the lessons they taught you. On the contrary, you will retain all you've learned from your past teachers—the ones you loved and the ones who hurt you. You will just stop carrying them around on your back. But first you must develop the skill of forgiveness.

The Sanskrit word for forgiveness is *kshama*. It translates literally to "capacity." When you allow your heart to open in love and become so big and bright that it eclipses the darkness, you have enlarged your capacity to create your future free from the ankle chains of regret, anger, guilt, and pain. Really and truly unshackling yourself from heartache is quite challenging. It requires courage and a willingness to endure the emotional intensity of letting go.

The good news is that the level of intensity will be much less than what you experienced in your past when you didn't have so many tools or as much knowledge of self. The Buddhist view of forgiveness is that it is really a decision you make to let go of your attachment to pain. Why isn't that easy to do?

So many people walk around carrying negative energy in a kind of autopilot mode because life is hard enough without dredging up old wounds even to let go of them. They also think that to forgive is to condone the actions of others, which isn't the case. You can let go of what's hurting you from any experience without agreeing with the unskilled choices of another. Perhaps you think you get along just fine from day to day without going there, right? But let me give you one very good reason to approach those past emotions again.

If you're still carrying anger, resentment, bitterness, judgment, insecurity, anxiety, overemotionality, or sensitivities, they will regularly throw you off center and taint your relationships with yourself and others. Every time these emotions pass through your body, it's like ingesting poison. Whether you're remembering something from high school or having yelled at the idiot driver this morning, you are drinking the poison right now. You feed it to those you love whenever you react from an old, untended wound. Carrying these feelings keeps the past from remaining in the past. It becomes a living negativity in the present, shadowing you every day, coloring all that you do and affecting your whole trip.

You might build up defenses to avoid a pain that you remember as being so overwhelming that to reawaken it may cause irreparable harm. By confronting the darkness that exists within your heart, however, you will discover that it is an illusion, something that you gave power to, and now you will take that power back and use it to create your life anew. In addition, you can begin to practice forgiveness in each moment, as things happen to you, so you can become more like the monk's master, who was immune to slights, and cease to collect more negativity as you walk along.

By forgiving (but not forgetting), you cease to be the victim of your past and gain mastery over your issues. I'm not saying it's easy, only that your true nature is more powerful than the shadows and armor we gather. Demons don't exist in us from birth; we put them there, and keep them alive, either consciously or unconsciously. They feel scary and strong, and they may be strong habits, but they are very weak at the root and easy to pull out with a little time and dedication. In the battle to win your soul, the only devil is you, and forgiveness will bring you victory over it.

Clear Your Mind

Though we have two to three thousand thoughts a day on average, scientists say it is possible to whittle that number down to about twelve hundred or so, and optimally, to mostly constructive or neutral ones. Yogis use meditation to take the garbage out of the mind and exist in the clarity and spaciousness left behind from this mental cleansing. Like its housework counterpart, taking out mental garbage has to be done on a regular basis to keep your inner state clean.

Your first task is to determine which negative thoughts are stuck on "repeat" throughout the day. Anything you think over and over will become more predominant in you as a belief, then as an emotion, and eventually as an action. This can be helpful: if you practice a yoga pose five times a week, you will get much more adept at it than if you do it, say, once a month. Now, imagine that you're doing that same yoga pose twenty-five hundred times a day, every day. That's what the mind is capable of.

Listen carefully today to your inner conversations. This is not the time for judging or editing; rather, allow yourself the freedom to simply listen and observe everything that passes through your mind. Notice that you have three main types of thoughts: positive, negative, and neutral, or filler, thoughts. Filler thoughts are the most common, and they constitute most of the mind's meaningless chatter. Of course, when you want to attract positive things into your life, you'll want to remove as many filler and negative thoughts as possible and let the positive ones remain.

Here in the weighing station, you have a new chance to literally rethink your life. You get to decide now what mental channels you will allow to be on repeat and which ones you need to switch off. You have an inner radio show host inside your head, one who is talking all the time. With practice, you will begin to notice when the chatter becomes counterproductive to the road you're on, and you can change the broadcast into what will help you travel smoothly.

For your thoughts to not have power over you, you should know that you can direct them at will and that they are not permanent. Think of your thoughts as clouds scudding across the sky. Notice they're there, but don't hang on to or worry about any of them. If you don't give them much energy (attention), they won't swell into storm clouds. If, however, you decide that your thoughts are who you are, then your sense of self and center will be whipped around with every fleeting thought-gust in your mind. You can begin clearing the cloudy mind by softening your attachment to any thought being inherently bad and, instead, see all thoughts as simply *happening*. Level the playing field by seeing every thought as equal, as one cloud is made of the same essence as another.

Thoughts are just energy, swirling around. It's what we give credence to, and what we do from there, that counts. To not react to them, and to allow them to exist as pure energy forms without any other value judgment attached, is a step toward mastering the little buggers. You are not on the quest to keep all of your thoughts around or to never think any, but if you are to unstick yourself from deep or meaningless thought patterns, you have to dissolve their power to move you from your goals, like, say, getting a good night's sleep.

When you see thoughts purely as a play of energy, they become raw materials for your creativity. Then you can begin to decide how to re-create, to reshape your thoughts anew. You can undo any thought, no matter how deep the habit of thinking it, and make it into any other form you want—you just have to learn how.

Anything that has held your environment, your mind, or your heart hostage—all material, mental, and emotional weight must be jettisoned if you are to make a fresh start. Take the wheel as you practice ways I've found to be most effective for getting rid of the old to welcome in the new on all three levels.

take the wheel
Making Space

You already know how to tidy up your house, your car, and your office—so I want you to do that as soon as possible. Then go deeper: call some friends today and schedule as many "clean machine" parties as there are people involved. Gather at one home each Sunday, for example, and everyone cleans and organizes for two hours. As the host, you'll give each person a job, so you'll know what's getting done and can make sure your nosy friend Gina stays out of your desk. Then afterward, go out or have dinner to celebrate together. Two hours can make a huge difference if five people are working together instead of one.

In yoga, we call helping others for free *seva*, or selfless service, and it is one way to make a conscious offering of your time and your elbow grease, which always gets you closer to your soul. For this reason, Zen practitioners think that peeling carrots is as good a path to spiritual awakening as prayer or meditation. No matter whether you're scrubbing your bathtub or someone else's, if you're doing it by choice, for the purpose of making space, then space will be made in all areas of your life as well.

Soji

All cultures value some type of space-clearing practice. One of my favorites is the Japanese art of *soji*, which means both house-cleaning and temple-cleaning, infusing the mundane act of housework with a sacred, ceremonial energy. You can do *soji* by mindfully tidying up for twenty minutes each morning, before doing anything else. After twenty minutes, stop and move on with your day.

Performing *soji* really means that by taking time to clean first thing in the morning, sweeping away dust, finishing the dishes from last night's dinner, or going deeper, through your hiding places, you are making a statement that today you're creating space and are ready and willing to receive your universal gifts that can now find a home in the places you've opened for them.

Make a list of all the areas you feel need *soji* attention, from changing the cat litter to going through old love letters. Whether you are naturally organized or not, your little daily ritual will cause you to create boundaries around your housework so you can get to the life's work at hand, yet it will, over time, make a serene mirror of the soul's Zen garden out of your living space.

The Three Steps of Letting Go

In a teaching that is parallel to the road trip ideals, feng shui principles show us three main steps to creating sacred space:

1. Remove anything that's blocking you or isn't representative of who you really are.

2. In-tend to your future—set your intentions for your space based on what you wish to magnetize toward you.

3. Embody those intentions through your conscious actions in every moment. This includes placing material things back into your space, only this time on purpose, for a purpose.

You can use these techniques anywhere, but start with the places where you spend the most time. Changing the energy matrix there will give you the most benefit.

The core focus of attracting what you want by clearing away what you don't want and re-creating your intimate spaces to vibe higher will be to remove anything that:

- Is not useful
- Takes up unnecessary space
- Causes feelings of negativity
- Is destructive to your soul's goals
- You don't like

Then, after you've set your intentions and envisioned what you want to surround yourself with, you can replace the removed items with new things that represent the same energy you wish to draw to you, anything that:

- Is useful
- Is sacred
- Causes feelings of positivity
- Is constructive to your soul's goals
- You love

On a sheet of paper, make a list with two columns: Stay or Go. Move around your house, and write down the major items that will definitely stay and those that will definitely go.

My good friend and feng shui master Ariel Towne says, "Before you can pick up something new, you have to put down what you're holding." So, what are you holding? Often, in my work, I find that people are afraid to let go of material things or even their outmoded relationships because they fear that they will never be able to replace them. In fact, the nature of energy is that it's compelled to fill a void. What you're doing now is mak-

Road Rule

Don't replace—upgrade.

ing sure that the void (space) is created, so you can then fill it with the experiences, people, and things that better reflect you.

This is a time for trust. When you create a void and do your work with awareness, you will soon see that place inhabited not with the same old stuff but with new things that cause you happiness and gratitude. Congratulations: you've traded up!

Feng Shui in Action

There are a whole lot of classical feng shui ways to orient your home. You can study the *bagua*, or the nine traditional areas that correlate to nine areas of your life, by reading books on the subject. One I recommend is *Move Your Stuff, Change Your Life* by Karen Rauch Carter. You'll learn what colors, elements, and objects to put in which area of your home. For our purposes here on the road trip, I want to show you the basic energetic foundations of feng shui in action. If you set your intentions powerfully at this underlying level, your choices will be in correct alignment with your soul, and they will resonate loud and clear.

As you sort through the past, which is what the items you hold onto represent, pay attention to the emotions and physical sensations you experience as you consider each item. The basic rule is this: If it makes you feel happy and loving now, keep it. If it feels laden with lack of interest, dislike, guilt, obligation, negativity, or anger, let it go immediately. The past is past.

Step 1: Decluttering

The first things to jettison are any negative, accumulated, or useless items. Go through your outer spaces and into drawers, piles, and closets, removing physical items that are of no use to you anymore. Look at each one. Hold it in your hands and reflect on the following questions:

- "When is the last time I used this?"
- "Is it serving me now in any positive way?"

If the answer is, "I may need this later," store the item away in an organized place. But if the answer is definitely, "No, this is no longer serving me," then the object let go. Donate it, sell it, or ceremonially sacrifice it to the Dumpster gods. If you're not going to use it, ask yourself why you're hanging on to it. Is it more important for you to keep this item around you, or to release the energy that it represents? Often, Ariel says, "We needed things in the past that served us well then, but now they don't." Know the difference.

Step 2: Intending

When you've cleared out all you can, add another level of intention about the way you want your life to be. This step takes you that extra mile toward your goals. Pause now to get a clear idea of which *you* you want your outer spaces to represent. Consult your map for orientation.

Step 3: Beautifying

Once you've made room, there will be holes, spaces to fill with the special things you need or love. If you need an item, make sure it serves you to get your house's work, your job's work, and your soul's work done, easily and well.

Your home is organized—now make it pretty. Add special touches, such as pictures, art, or meaningful mementos that serve as symbolic reminders of what it is to live your greatest possible life.

Perhaps you will set up a meditation area where you place items that inspire you, frame your own photographs for your walls, or keep fresh flowers on the table. If you have a partner or kids, decide together what goes into this step. What's going on in your shared space reflects what's going on in everyone's hearts, so make it an inspired and inspiring reflection.

Clearing Your Inner State

As you begin to match your outer space to your greatest intentions, the next frontier is to go deeper inside, to face your mind and heart clutter. We'll start with actions that literally clear your head. The rewards are great: you will develop more focus and follow through on any project you undertake, and you will be able to choose a cool, a calm approach when thoughts, worries, and questions do arise.

What follows are a few simple techniques that will have a big, positive effect on your mental state. Make them a part of each day, or use them as needed when you feel as if things between your ears are getting a little overwhelming.

Sandstorm Meditation

I've been doing the Sandstorm Meditation since I was a child in order to fall asleep. This creative meditation technique reveals the true nature of your thoughts and the power you have over them. It can instantly make you aware of how feeble your negative thoughts are when they are confronted by the strength of your positive intentions. The Sandstorm Meditation reminds me of the process of creating and destroying the sand mandala that is used in Tibetan Buddhist rituals. A sand mandala is an intricate, circular pattern made using colored sand, and is intense and beautiful to behold in its symmetry. It may take monks weeks, even months or years, to make one mandala. After a time of ceremony and contemplation, the mandala is destroyed by being swept away and the sand returned to the earth. This ritual symbolizes the shifting nature of all things.

The point of living is believed to be for the pure joy of creating and experiencing the fullness of love, alongside the realization that nothing you create, be it relationships, careers, accumulation of things, or even your thoughts themselves, will last in the way you now know it. Everything evolves and changes form, except love, which is constant, and the nature of your soul. Knowing this in advance can keep you in full gratitude for the precious yet transient moment at hand.

This meditation can keep any and all thoughts at bay, so you can float for a moment in the space of no-thought, an experience that many traditions consider a most advanced state of being. The following instructions will show you how you can uncreate, re-create and redirect your thought-energy, anytime you choose.

1. Find an easy, comfortable seat on the floor or a chair, or lie down. Breathe deeply using your *ujjayi* breathing for one to two minutes. Then relax your breath, close your eyes, and begin.

2. First, envision your thoughts—either every thought if you want to try the no-thought mode, or just negative thoughts specifically—as being made of sand.

3. When they come into your awareness, choose your mode of making them disappear—watching them fly apart like sand in the wind, dissolve and pour to the ground as if in an hourglass, be swept away by a big broom in your mind, hit the fan of your awareness and be scattered—any visualization that works for you.

4. You can also reconstitute the sand-thought back into its original form or into another, completely different thought. Try to see what you can create and destroy and create anew, and you will quickly understand that this power is, and has been, yours all along.

Here is my favorite scenario: I'm driving through the desert. It's windy. I turn on the windshield wipers while I drive. Whenever a sand-thought hits my windshield, it dissolves in a burst and gets instantly wiped away. Visualizing my thoughts helps me remain in my center more easily, to imagine it as the inside of my car, where I'm safe, immune from the sandstorm of thought and emotion. This meditation lets me chill out and keep most thoughts at bay when my mind is speeding along and nothing else will slow it down.

With practice, it won't take as much concentration to sand-ify each thought, but instead you will develop a thought buffer inside your mind that you can call into action whenever you wish. Dissolving unwanted or harmful thoughts and replacing them with those that help you will become easier and easier. Once you see that your thought-energies are malleable, you can have fun sweeping them out or shaping them into whatever form you choose next.

Start a Meditation Revolution

Meditation is a mind-centering technique known and practiced by every major spiritual tradition. In the West, it's gaining popularity, and it's no longer uncommon to hear someone tell you she missed your call because "I've just been meditating."

To meditate on something is to reflect within, to pay attention inwardly, past body, mind, and emotions—all the way into your soul. You don't have to be a monk to meditate or sit for hours. Even a few minutes spent in any way that allows you some time and space to be in the moment, commune with your Inner Teacher, and get in touch with your highest intentions is a very powerful way to get more fluent in "center"speak.

There is a multitude of ways you can meditate, but it's generally agreed that the best position is a comfortable, cross-legged pose, or sitting in a chair with your feet on the floor. It's said in many traditions that the energy centers of the body attune much easier when the spine is upright. If you're unable to sit still at length and can lie on your back without falling asleep, this position is acceptable, too.

Meditation is awesome, because you can get major benefits from it instantly. You don't need years of study to reflect within; rather, this experience of sitting with your calm, abiding center is quite natural to you. You just need to allow it. You're simply entering into a process of recalling how easy it is. If you haven't done it in a while, you may feel rusty. But keep going—it's like riding a bike. It will all come back to you.

The Highway Meditation

I don't know about you, but I, and every other type A personality I know, could use a regular dose of being here instead of being everywhere else. Fear is one of the biggest mind-clutterers there is, yet it is most often found elsewhere—in thoughts of the past or the future—but is rarely found in the present. Learning to live more often in the now rewards you with a greater ability to live fearlessly and make the courageous choices that will lead you into more freedom of the heart and mind.

Anytime you are in an active state of expectation—for instance, hearing the car pull into the driveway and knowing a good friend you haven't seen in years is about to walk through the door—you are in a state of pure present-moment awareness. You are fully in the now, and when this happens, your soul takes over, unimpeded by the usual roadblocks of confusion, fear, or anxiety. You may then experience bursts of inspiration, epiphanies, creativity, or feelings of love, compassion, and understanding.

All of these energy bursts arise from the soul, your highest sense of being. Fear can block our heart's freedom—and fear is at the root of every stressful thought or need to obsessively search through the past and the future to make sure we don't experience more pain and disappointment. The ego is terrified of your being here, being clear, and getting your soul's work done. It isn't needed in the clarity of the present, so to survive, it compels you to faux–time travel to other, imaginary places where it feels more important.

To quickly return to the moment at hand, try the Highway Meditation:

1. Imagine you're sitting somewhere peaceful and calm. Make the scenery anything you wish—I like the blooming desert at springtime. You're on a lounge chair, enjoying the sun on your face and listening to the sounds of the moment. Notice as much sensory detail as you can, to bring your vision into full color. Maybe you've got a song playing; there's a light, sandy wind tickling your legs; or a tiny blue-striped lizard is darting into the shade underneath your chair. What do you feel, see, hear, smell, or taste? Out in front of you, distant enough to be safe but close enough to hear the engine drone of the cars that pass, is a highway. Each car that drives by represents a single thought. Depending on your inner state, there may be a lot of cars or very few.

2. Bring yourself into a state of expectation now. Instead of watching the cars pass, begin to wait in anticipation for the next one. Become interested and say to yourself, "I wonder when the next car is going to pass." When it does,

immediately repeat the statement and wait excitedly for the next car to come by. When it does, watch it zoom past and disappear, then immediately begin waiting for the next one. Don't judge the thought-cars. Just let them pass, then anticipate the next.

3. You will notice that when you are in the experience of waiting for a car, the vehicles will begin to pull apart, and there will seem to be more time and space in between. The same thing happens with your thoughts. By bringing yourself into the moment, you are making spaces among your thoughts for your soul to pour forth with abundance. In the places in between, you are immersing in the source energy from which all thoughts come and to which they will return.

4. Come back to the highway meditation any time you need to center into the now. It's highly effective in times of emotional reactivity, creative blocks, when you need inspiration, when you have trouble falling asleep, or when you just need to get grounded. You may notice more soul connection happening even after the meditation ends.

This technique also works, strangely, to cure the hiccups. If you pretend that the hiccups are cars instead of thoughts, after a couple of minutes the hiccups will disappear.

Heart Clearing

One of the best ways to lighten the emotional load on your heart is to practice forgiveness. I will now teach you the three-step process to really, truly let go.

One major definition of *forgive* is "to cease to feel resentment against." Another is "to give up all claim against." By forgiving your past, you literally give it back to itself.

By hanging on to any negative part of the past, you are allowing people from that time to crowd in here with you, and that suffocating energy will persist in all your present relationships with yourself and others, continuing to cause harm and sorrow until you send it packing.

Students of the soul experience something that may feel confusing, hurtful, or disappointing, and the first thing they say is not, "Why me?" or "Why are you doing this to me," but "Thank you." They thank the uni-

Road Rule

Whatever you hold onto, you will eventually act out—and you will act *in*, against yourself. Do not give others that power. Send the past back to the past.

verse, their highest knowing for the invitation to practice, to know themselves better, to set a boundary, or move in a different direction. And then they set about doing what is needed with a hardy strength of spirit.

It's easy to say, "Thank you" when you receive a gift on the other side of a hard time. It builds more inner power, however, to say it right smack in the middle.

Take some time today and write a letter to the person or people in your life you thought you could never forgive for what they did. You will forgive them, not just for their benefit but for yours. You forgive so as to say your final, loving no to them: "No, you will no longer have the power to be destructive to me, or to my loving relationships. No, you cannot remain in my intimate space. I free myself through compassion for you. I will not allow you to enter here again."

Here's an exercise to help you learn how to have the direct experience of deep and lasting forgiveness and finally, wholly, put the heavy past down and walk away.

The Three-Step Forgiveness Exercise

1. Forgive the person, not necessarily the act. Whether people are still in your life or not, you can have compassion for them and their mistakes without condoning their actions.

Forgiveness and agreement are not the same thing. Separate them by reflecting on the following statements:

- As a fellow human being who falters, I forgive you your unskilled choices. I send light to you and wish you peace on your journey.

- As a divine being who shares the deepest source connection with you, I honor you at the highest level for what you really are, although you may not know it or act from this place.

- As my own person who is moving into alignment with what I need, I disagree with some of your choices and release myself from them. I give myself the right to move on, freed from all bonds between us.

2. Forgive yourself. Perhaps you hold anger or guilt for unskilled choices you made. Remember that you did not have the tools you have now. As the more awake and aware person you are today, send light and love to who you were. Stop chastising yourself and continuing to punish yourself for old decisions through your habits and actions. Honor the lessons you've learned by doing things differently now, and that includes treating yourself with increased dignity, understanding, and compassion.

3. Tear down the wall. Whenever you hold on to the past in a negative way, it becomes a wall erected in defense of further pain, and against others. This wall is really your unwillingness to come to terms with what happened and is a resistance to moving forward. If there's a wall in your way, you can't take even one step ahead. Imagine tearing it down. You can set limits and choose not to further relate with this person or repeat the same missteps you took in the past. But you don't need to hold up a wall to do this, especially a wall whose weight you are holding all by yourself. Let it crumble, and enjoy the energetic boomerang of release as it comes back to you in every way.

Drop-It Meditation

To avoid future negativity becoming stuck to you, anytime you undergo an upsetting experience you have trouble shaking, do this simple exercise to clear it:

1. Sit in a comfortable posture.

2. Close your eyes and begin to breathe slowly and deeply through your nose.

3. After you feel settled, turn your awareness to your heart. What have you been carrying there that feels negative, constrictive, heavy? What have you not been able to forgive? Perhaps a person will come to mind; perhaps an event that occurred.

4. Envision a beautiful, magical room into which you can enter. Decorate it as you wish so it is a safe place of self and light.

5. You hear a knock on your door. Open it, and invite in the person or experience that you wish to forgive. Sit at the table with him or her. Offer the person a cup of tea. You don't need to become the person's best friend, but you do need to know him or her a little better.

6. Really look at this person, and see if you can perceive him or her as a human, fallible being who was simply not acting in alignment, probably unknowingly. "Forgive them, for they know not what they do," a wise man once said. Most people think they're doing something constructive, something the best way they know how—even though they may fall far short as far as you're concerned.

7. Perhaps you need to have a conversation with this person. Imagine expressing everything you need to, and at the end of the conversation, when you're ready, hand over a box, inside which is the negative energy you've been holding onto around the relationship. Watch the individual take it back, lift the top, and see a swirl of dark energy fly up

and away, out an open window, turning back into golden light as it joins the universal source. Now you are both free from what bound you.

8. On every exhale now, begin to feel that energy, person, or event exiting your body, mind, and heart. In your room, firmly and politely ask this person to leave. Follow him or her to the door, and say your good-byes. Then close the door.

9. Open your eyes and be where you are for a few moments, then get up and continue your day. You'll be lot lighter now.

Pay attention to how you feel as you go through this exercise. Old emotions such as anger, fear, numbness, even laughter and tears may arise. That's normal. Keep breathing, for at least five minutes, with your mind attuned to the intention to let go—and you will.

Once your heart is clearer, spend a few minutes reflecting on this thought: Can you now trust that the release of the experience you needed to forgive, whatever it has been or will be, is meant for your highest good and that of those around you? Look into your past—can you see how this has been true when in the moment you were feeling only pain? That later all became clear, and you were thankful for it? If you can come to truly believe this, you are ready to surrender the hardness, self-loathing, victim mentality, defenses, disappointments, pain, and excessive control. It's your room, and no one gets in whom you don't want to join you there.

If you knew in advance what you were here to experience, you might not invest in the moment as fully. How much would a breakup hurt if you knew it was leading you toward the love of your life? Not that much. Yet you must go through heartbreak to strengthen and mold your heart in the way that will fit your soul mate. In that case, what, ultimately, is so bad about that breakup? I'd say it's so good. Sometimes we require ourselves to feel lost, to inspire us to seek and then find the deeper answers that lead us into that next level of our being. Just maybe, your past made you who you are and gave you tools you can use to have the best life ever. And would you trade that? Knowing that your past transformed you into the wise, resilient person you are today can help you soften, and humbly say to the moment, "I don't know the outcome, but I trust it is for my best." Then you can stop wanting your past to be different from what it was, and see the real love behind the higher experiences you received from your soul's guides.

Lighten up, and as you drive on, now with less junk in your trunk, you can allow what you don't understand to draw you closer to center and find all the ways available to drop the past and get back to love. Make the choices that keep you aligned and moving forward as the strong, capable you that you are—right here and now.

the tunnel of love

How to Have a Lifelong Love Affair with Yourself

my trip
A Personal Affair

It was a lonely night in Butte, Montana, and I'd spent the entire day feeling roadsick. (An all-too-common malady that causes perfectly independent road trippers to begin searching outside themselves for someone else to complete them, roadsickness strikes suddenly and with few warning signs, causing its victims to arbitrarily increase the interest factor placed upon people—any people—due to discomfort at the thought of being alone). I decided to hole up in my motel room and concoct a makeshift yet calming bubble bath with a travel-size bottle of shampoo and lavender gas-station potpourri. I realized after bursting into tears when the shampoo wasn't foamy enough that I wanted someone there with me to share the bath, the moment, and make me feel needed. I grabbed myself in a hug out of frustration, then stopped. I had an epiphany, right there in the pine-scented bathroom: I could hold my *own* hand, hug *myself,* pour *myself* a glass of water at night, give *me* my own *New York Times* arts section at breakfast, or do any number of things that I thought I needed someone else around to do. It even felt pretty much the same! I was thirty years old and had never noticed that I was one of my soul mates—the one who is the most like me I'd ever meet. I raised my clasped hands and shook them like a referee calling a boxing match. "Tonight," I yelled triumphantly, "I am my own boyfriend!"

The couple next door pounded on the wall at me, but I didn't even care. I toweled off and put on my best cowgirl outfit, and for effect I added a Cindy Crawford–like mole with black eyeliner. Then I took myself out on the town.

It was one of the best dates I've ever had. I knew exactly what I wanted and didn't have to listen to one boring story about somebody's exes or love of ice-fishing. When I was ready to do something else, I left for it immediately. I even thought I sang "Ring of Fire" like a total country star in the bar's karaoke event.

By the end of the night, I'd had three different cowboys ask to make me dinner, breakfast, and everything in between. But each time, I just laughed, pointed at myself, and said, "Sorry, I'm with her!"

I'm interested in nothing less than you finding true love. Before your road trip is over, you will know exactly how to choose the relationships that can bring you to this wonderful place in your heart. But before you *get* love, you must learn how to *give* it, to yourself, without anyone else's help. Your lifelong affair with you begins here, with this realization: when you disregard your own heart, you open the channel for the same from the outside world.

Road Rule

The way to be in love is to *be* love.

If there are still areas of yourself where you are not in near-total loving acceptance of who you are, then you are still sending out a partial signal that says, "I am not worthy." And, depending on its strength, you will continue to attract people and situations that prove to you that you are not lucky in love.

So many people long for a great relationship and look for it outside of themselves. They find a loving partner. They throw themselves into loving the other person and, in so doing, forget themselves and give their stability to the other person to control. Then, when that one-way energy dissipates, they chase it and eventually lose the beautiful thing they once had. This is the worst-case scenario, one you can stop creating in your life. You never again need lose your ground or your ability to generate happiness and self-confidence whether in or out of partnership. Drawing in and self-generating love at all times is the only answer. At my favorite coffee shop in Brooklyn, their tip jar has a lid painted with a big smile, and that's where you slide in your dollar bills. The sign reads, "Feed the Happy," which is what you do every time you take another action that enriches your heart. In this chapter, I will teach you how to feed the happy so you need never feel empty-hearted again.

The amount of acceptance, understanding, empathy, and reverence you have for yourself directly affects how fully you can give to or receive from another person. To better orient you to the primary affair that you must cultivate if you wish to be independent, strong, and fierce of heart, you'll need the map.

the map
Your Heart Is Like a Tire

As we begin our tunnel of love adventure, it may be helpful to know that no matter what happens to your heart, it can never actually be broken. What is the heart, really? It can be explained in three parts, which actually all work together to form your whole experience of love.

We have a physical heart located in the chest; when we're anxious or upset, we release chemicals in our brain that cause us to feel such physical sensations as pain or palpitations. We also have an emotional heart that experiences the swirling winds of our feelings, which can also cause physical discomfort or pleasure. We can neither see nor touch this heart, yet at the emotional level, we do feel the searing pain of heartbreak and the soaring heights of passion. There is a third, deeper heart in us all, and it's found at the soul level.

At its essence, your heart is whole, untouched by pain, and as pristine as that of anyone else's. Yoga philosophers call this *anahata*, or the "unstruck place." If you've ever touched that calm center, even as you go through heartbreak or tragedy, you know what I'm talking about. In many spiritual teachings, the *anahata* is the seat of our true compassion, and the center of our equilibrium. It's akin to a quiet country road on a still summer morning. It's in you, and you can walk that road whenever you desire.

You must learn to find this path, and tread upon it, whether you have external relationships or not, in order to be in love with your life. This doesn't mean you have to neglect or stop wanting to be in partnerships while you undergo this process, but it does mean you'll develop the power to truly love—yourself, and therefore others, courageously and without regret.

Think of your heart as a tire. It has outer layers: the place where the rubber meets the road. These layers, which correlate to the physical layer, take all the heat. They are affected by the energy of friction and can change shape with the intensity of usage, even to the point of an eventual breakdown. Going further inside, there is the center structure of the tire and the air it contains. This is your emotional layer—affected by the pressures of the outside. Even if this layer feels flat once in a while, it can be easily refilled. At the core of a tire, in the deepest place, there is a rim made of steel. The innermost place in your heart is like that—cool and strong enough to hold up through the fiercest intensity. This place is the still point of many Eastern philosophies, and to know it is to live from center, unwavered by either the petty or the big dramas of life.

When you feel strong reactions, such as fear, pain, or insecurity, it's easy to believe that they are your only reality. In the moment, such intensity can be overwhelming. Yet when you realize that reactions and the emotions they bring forth are not all of you—they are only momentary heat and pressure afflicting the outer layers of your being—you can stop, realign by remembering your deepest unstruck place, and begin to take action from there to resist a misalignment that could throw you more permanently off course.

The fastest route to your heart's core is to fall. You'll have to fall in love with yourself, maybe for the first time, or perhaps you're just renewing your vows. Either way, what the tunnel of love asks of you is to begin making a daily commitment that will lead to you love being with yourself, to truly enjoy your own company. When you become happy on your own, then no one or no other thing can ever have more power over your heart than you do. That's because you'll know that whatever happens with another party, you will survive and, not only that, you'll prosper. This is a simple but profound state that the most healthy, independent people have attained. It benefits every relationship you have now or will have, if you can come to it undefended and fearless because you are no longer afraid to be alone.

Even when you have developed a consistent love affair with yourself, you will still feel temporary sensations of suffering at the outer level of your heart. Everyone does. If you can remember that pain is but an outer illusion, however, then, like peeling back the layers of a tire until the steel shines through, you will discover the strength inside to deal with anything that comes.

The Ego

It's easy to say you're ready for something great to come into your life, like that perfect relationship, life's work, friends, and so forth, without first having an equally healthy relationship with yourself.

This contradiction is the energetic pothole of wanting one thing but acting in opposition to that wish. If you don't have a strong and healthy relationship with yourself, you may find yourself attracting love that peters out over time, or feel unable to fully participate in that love if you do get it.

I invite you to first draw inside, to the spaces in yourself that perhaps you've looked to others to fill. We all have that feeling of emptiness, of not being enough, of not being loveable. Insecurities and fear occur at the level of your ego, that part of the tire that is rubber and air, not steel.

I do not think the ego is only in our mind. I believe it is a holistic state of our being, one that helps us relate to the outer world and designate our place in it. It tells us why we're different or unique: "I am a yoga teacher. I have red hair. I am the oldest child." And on and on. The ego is how we delineate our individuality in the world. But living only from the ego can cause you to feel cut off, separate from others, and, therefore, overly affected by their perceptions, actions, and choices. Since love is unity, and the ego needs an illusion of division to exist, working only from the ego won't help you to love.

The problem with the outer layers of ego is that they are unstable. Since the ego needs separateness to exist, it is afraid of unity; instead, it will show you the differences—in opinion, in motive—and lead you to feel disconnected from others. All arguments come from ego.

The outer layers exist in a constant state of instant gratification, wanting to be recognized as a separate entity—and if union with others gets close, they may change their tactics irrationally from one moment to the next, anything to prove that you are an individual, that you are not interconnected with all living beings. As a result, your inner voice says, "You don't do that right," and other external-directed criticisms such as "I'm not as pretty as her" and various inner self-worth issues arise.

Acting from your ego, you can still make choices but not from your deepest *anahata* place of clarity and wisdom. So you may get what your ego wants but not what you really need to be happy. You might attract money, the Lamborghini, the guy, the pool. But there will be little heart in these things, and therefore the love may be absent from your life.

The ego is not always cranky. It is changeable because sometimes it's good to be resilient, to go with the flow. This is how personal evolution happens. It's also good to be distinctive, and to have something unique to offer the world.

However, if you think the outer layers are all that you are, as Buddha said, you will live a life of suffering, tossed everywhere on the ever-changing and stormy seas of experience. Things will always seem to change, but that suffering will never end. No audience in the world that will give you enough applause. No one will love you enough. You must know how to travel from the ego, and its obsession with getting validation inorganically from the outside, to the inner self, where validation is something you self-generate naturally.

Moving In

We love to proclaim, "But I know exactly what I want in a relationship!" "I deserve true love and to be treated with the ultimate respect!" "I am worthy of total love and compassion!"

Pause for a moment, though, and ask yourself, "Am I consistently treating myself in the same wonderful ways that I expect from all my other healthy relationships? Do I react to my own shortcomings and learning process with as much compassion and understanding as I treat other people?" If you answered yes, good job! But if you're like most people, then the honest answer is, "Not really."

The secret of the ego, or the outer layers of your heart, is that it is meant to be a translation tool between you and the world, yet it ends up leading us to believe that we are only what we prefer. Our preferences are not who we really are, however, *especially* when those preferences are negative or destructive to our well-being. We confuse our preferences when we believe things that harm our sense of self-love, or place our sole happiness in the hands of specific people and forget our inner practice. It's good to want things—but it's not good to want them so much that you cannot stay centered and strong if you lose them. This is when a choice becomes a chokehold.

If you remain stuck at the outer layers of your heart, you'll be unsure about whether you can handle being alone. This leads to too much emphasis and dependence on people outside of you, and every relationship will collapse under this kind of weight. If you do not have your own resources at the deepest level, how can you expect anyone else to take over for you? They can't, even if they want to—not for very long, anyway.

So let's move inside, to the soul, and go from merely tolerating your alone time until you can be with someone else to really, truly adoring time spent with yourself. That's where the root of true love begins to take hold.

We attract the people to us who reflect the relationship we're having with ourselves. There can be no other way for the universe except to give you what you're asking for through doing. Love, like any other energy, follows a circular motion of giving you back the same vibration you're sending out.

There are two kinds of love circles: the one where you give love to yourself and then offer it out into your world in the form of loving words, thoughts, and actions; and the one where you have a partner and you give and receive from each other simultaneously.

Most people, however, see only one kind of circle—the one linking them to someone else. If they have it, they feel good, and if they don't, they feel drained and miss the life infusion that loving another brings them. Many people don't realize they can infuse themselves by loving solo.

To not practice loving yourself is giving up the driver's seat and letting someone else dictate your happiness, a situation we must swerve to avoid here on the road trip. It becomes dangerous if you are not aware of your capacity to feel love independently of others. Depression, anxiety, neediness, dysfunction, desperation, codependency, and even self-harming actions can occur.

Remember now your ability to create a personal circle of love, one that will, like a wedding band, signify unity with your soul forever, and fuel your heart every day of your life. In fact, go out and get a beautiful ring to symbolize your lifelong commitment to this bond of self.

It's Not about You Unless You Decide It Is

The whole world is an infinite field of possibility. Things happen that may seem outside your choosing, because your reality bumps into someone else's all the time, and although you can have an influence, you can't control what someone else decides to do. But from the moment you have an interaction with another individual, the way you see things and your choice of actions from there on *is* entirely under your direction.

The strategies in this section will help free you from taking other people's choices—even the most scary, awful ones—personally, and let you get back to your heart center, where you can make better decisions, free from the drag of disempowerment.

Let's say your partner doesn't roll the toothpaste tube from the bottom up but instead squeezes it from the middle and then leaves the cap off, creating a minty mess all over the sink. This drives you nuts, and you have had multiple arguments about it. Your partner is perplexed: none of his or her other partners gave a hoot about the toothpaste.

This example shows what people in relationships mean when they say, "It's not about you—it's about me." This cliché sounds like a cop-out for exiting a relationship or choosing some action that upsets you, but the meaning behind it is actually valid.

Road Rule

To take on something another person thinks as a statement of your inherent worthlessness is to misalign. To realize that your worthiness stands regardless of another's opinions, preferences, or actions is to become a master.

You need to understand this concept to release your reactivity to others' choices and get back to the work of loving yourself.

One person will detest that you talk about your friends all the time. The next person will think it's great that you have a close relationship with your friends and will love you more because of it. One boyfriend will fall head over heels in love with you; the next one will leave because he never fell in love with you. One guy will say, "Sorry—I like my women thinner." Does this mean you are not attractive the way you are? Absolutely *not*, because you'll meet someone else who will love your curves. I know more than one woman who developed eating issues after just one man thought she was too big for his tastes. I want you to avoid that kind of selective power transfer at all costs.

Knowing that preferences are specific to the person having them, and that every person is different, you can begin to cease generalizing and to heal from the idea that you are inherently *anything* but what you want to be. Let's move this same concept inside.

We each have a running commentary in our head. Sometimes it's positive but, often, self-defeating, angry, doubtful, or otherwise destructive thoughts keep us from acting from a strong sense of self. You may think you love yourself just fine, but what if you did something clumsy and your partner said, "You're such an idiot!" to you? Someone would be sleeping on the couch. Maybe someone else's couch. Yet you may find that you're tolerating similar behavior and even these same words from yourself.

When it comes to the running commentary you have about yourself, listen closely. What beliefs do you hold about who you are, based on feedback from other people? Which parts are you not okay with, or embarrassed about, even? Are there still facets you're ashamed of—that you find weak or unpalatable to others, based on your fears or past comments you've received?

When asked, 99 out of 100 people will say, "Yes, I am worthy of being loved for who I am," but the voices inside your head might be saying something different. When you begin to realize that truth is relative to the observer, yet your self-worth is always under your control, you can begin not only to shift your perceptions of yourself to more empowering ones, but you can release some of the past pain of the grandiose ideas about what's "wrong" with you that were actually just built around another person's opinion.

Continuing to strengthen unloving thought patterns from within is a dead-end street. It can lead to self-loathing, insecurity, and obsessive worrying, and even become the downfall of some relationships—or at least your strength and happiness while you're in them. You may have started with one person's opinions of you, but your choosing to sustain a belief in them has led you to act in ways that continue to prove yourself right. It may seem like this proof is coming from the outside, but, in fact, you are instrumental in generating it and then allowing it to be perpetuated.

From now on, you will know your value and respectfully agree to disagree with anyone who says otherwise.

Your Thoughts Can Be Rerouted

It's strange. You may want to love yourself better. You may dive into mantras or spiritual practices that begin to change the way you look at yourself. You're getting back to loving who you are, and your happiness is increasing, when all of a sudden, wham! The same old mean voices appear, to dampen your joy. This happens to all of us, just so you know. It happened to Jesus and Gandhi and Mother Teresa and everyone else in the world. Self-doubt and its partner, self-criticism, are great ways to break the circle of love. We may never be able to fully silence our destructive voices, but we can create a new truth that drains them of their power.

This negative voice gets stronger more often, the more you allow it to speak or don't counteract it when it does. For years, you may have told yourself, "I am incapable of intimacy," "I am an angry person," "I attract drama like a high school thespian," and so on. It will take a while to rewire the electrical connections, but it's possible.

I love the book *The Hidden Messages of Water* by Masaru Emoto. In it, he took hundreds of water samples from rivers, lakes, and taps around the world. He then poured the ones from the same sources into various containers. The water crystals looked exactly alike—until people started talking to them. The ones receiving positive comments—"I love you," "You're beautiful," and the like—transformed into a beautiful structure, aligned and perfect. The ones getting the negative comments—"I hate you," "I want to kill you," and so forth—turned into a disgusting form akin to a cigarette burn on a yellow couch. There was no explainable reason for this, except for the change in intention (energy) moving through them.

You are 70 percent water. What you tell yourself, and allow those around you to tell you about yourself, affects you to the core. So watch what you say and accept from others. Make your behavior positively transformative by beginning with how you regard yourself.

Reinventing You

A friend once told me about one of his close buddies who had recently passed away. The man, a student of life, spent his time on earth doing diverse jobs, from photography to painting to working with space missions. He was able to be a success in each of these areas and many more. When people doubted his ability to just switch and be a painter, or remarked on the way he could just fearlessly pick up and try something new, he would always smile and say, "You are not what you do." He realized that the outer work was an extension of his inner being, yet one particular career did not define his true nature.

His story taught me also that at the level of the soul you are one thing, yet at the level of your choices, you can act like quite another. This same very wise man smoked intensely and eventually died of lung cancer.

You are not what you do, yet choice matters: some people choose life-affirming actions, and some choose negative actions, engaging in painful, self-limiting behaviors. Each affects your life's outcome.

Remember still that nothing you do is who you really are, whether it be picking up a beer or a glass of water, yelling at someone you love or treating the person with respect, staying in an abusive relationship or leaving it, and all the other myriad things you could choose. Who you really are at the soul level is an energetic superstore containing the basic energy from which you could form every possible thought, emotion, and action. Each of us has the potential to choose the most uplifting action, or the most horrible one. Though you may have a few traits of your body and personality that don't change much over a lifetime (for example, your height and your eye color), the things you choose to think, say, and do are all under your creative power, and once you do them, they define you to the outside world. It's through your actions that you manifest your destiny, and that destiny will absolutely be altered depending not on who you are, but on what you chose to *do* with it.

It is key to realize that at the soul level, this pre-action energy of being is not bad or good, or even constructive or destructive. It is neutral, available, in all forms. It just *is.* Yoga philosophy describes this soul, and the connection to the creative source it represents, as Shiva energy—that which simply exists, without movement. Shakti is the name for what happens when we move this energy through our choices, intentions, and deeds. In this way, how you decide to draw from the source, and which behaviors you pick, can either build up your experience of love and alignment or block you from it.

A key to loving yourself is to understand that what you do habitually becomes your outer costume of who you are, but who you really are is nonaction, or what the Buddhists call "emptiness." You will become however you decide to think, feel, and act. What you can decide to become is limitless. Your choices of how to express your soul's energy in this lifetime are infinite. This knowledge should make you reverent toward the immense importance of your life. You are here as a great artist of spirit and humanity, and with the art work you make of yourself, you can inspire. Choose according to your greatest vision, and you will become that. When you begin to see your own masterful power and reveal your latent majesty, you will begin to spark the love of self from within.

Our biggest mistake as humans is to look at our destructive, habitual patterns and think we cannot choose again, because we have fallen prey to the illusion that what we have chosen repeatedly is who we are stuck with being. When you become superglued to your choices, and think you are the one who lacks—the Drinker, the Smoker, the One Who Can't Find a Good Man, the Angry Guy or Girl, the Abuse-Collector, the Weak, the Oversensitive, the Unlovable One, and on and on—you've made a grave error that will cost you your true life.

You always have the power—and the *right*—to choose again or differently, if you want. Before you make that decision, however, know this: Choices are either constructive or destructive to your happiness. They either help you gain life energy or drain it. Knowing beforehand which choices will cause energy *gain* is important to the success of your ongoing relationship with yourself and the ultimate success of your road trip.

Road Rule

Choose love for gain—and
lack for pain.

Your Shadow Side

Loving is actually easy. The ability to love exists within us as our organic foundation. The real work of loving yourself and others is to remove the lid we all keep over love in varying degrees of closure. That lid is fear: fear of being hurt, fear that we won't survive more pain, and fear of exposing our whole heart and having it be rejected by someone we love. This fear is valid, since heartbreak does happen. Yet we can wage a sweet battle against this fear, which becomes irrelevant when you are able to remain in a state of inner loving no matter who loves you back, who rejects you, or who stays.

So let's take the lid off, and like a jar of fireflies released into the night, let your natural state of love fly free, making everyone who sees it squeal in delight at its miraculous luminescence. To do this, you must be able to recognize, confront, and win against your fear. Fear changes form often. You may experience it as insecurity, self-doubt, anger, stress, and many more emotions I call the shadows. The shadows have gotten a bad reputation in some circles, with students trying to avoid them so as to be "spiritual."

Feeling good is not the only aim of a truly soul-connected practice. Being able to transmute both your shadows *and* light into aligned action is. When you are able to navigate the middle place between positive and negative and come to a place of focus and wisdom, you are said to be at center. So often, people live only at polarities: they seek total bliss all the time, and when they find it fleeting, they swing into depression, confusion, and aimlessness. The challenge is to stay at center, in the unstruck place, regardless of what energies are confronting you.

Feeling intimacy can be just as great a challenge to your inner equilibrium as can feeling terrible. When you receive a strongly bad feeling, such as anger or fear, the tendency is to do anything to make it go away, but we also do this with strongly good experiences. Many people don't see where they use fear-based walls to block themselves from receiving the positive. Doing so would mean that they have to agree that they deserve such great things, and fear doesn't like this. The only way to become whole in your heart is to use every strong emotion, thought and experience and alchemize them into what empowers love rather than denies it. Transforming your shadows into center is the goal.

You'll take actions later on to bring you into direct connection with this lesson. For now, I want to introduce you to a new way of seeing all those things about yourself you might not like, or like to feel.

If the soul contains all forms of energy, then pushing discomfort away as undesirable is to deny part of your very nature and also cut yourself off from half of your creative options. Let me make this clear: nothing is inherently bad unless you decide it is and act as such.

Shadows are, in fact, a necessary part of our wholeness and can help guide us through our spiritual journeys, as well as our lives. For example, anger is a powerful energy that can show us where we are not in alignment or agreement. Yet anger is not inherently destructive, unless we act it out in a destructive way. Until then, we can use the power of anger to propel us into action, such as to sponsor a child when we feel indignant about the poverty of the world. *Tapas*, or properly channeled angry determination, is the fuel for many a yogi's breakthrough on the mat. It is also known as purification. Your use of the fire of intense emotional energy can either light your way or burn the moment into lifeless ash. It all depends on you.

The shadows are often misunderstood, and when you see them as not spiritual or not loving and try to push them away, ignore them, or act out because of them, you'll just create a monster.

Let me clarify this point. It's not the shadow emotion itself that diminishes you, that makes you look bad, disappoint yourself, or feel weak, or causes people to give you negative feedback about your behavior—it's your choice of how you used the shadows' energy that caused any of that. When you let the shadows have the power to make you angry, reactive, and dramatic; when you start blaming others and lashing out; you have chosen to act destructively. When you react, you have stepped away from the flow of abundance and well-being. You will not feel good. This is usually why we detest the shadows: because they are very hard to endure, and so you may try to dump them out into the situation, rather than sitting with the discomfort and waiting until you can direct the energy toward actions that have integrity.

No one likes being dumped on. Therefore, you may get the message from those around you that the shadows are not okay to admit to or to show people. You may have begun to see them as unacceptable parts of you and learned to keep them covered up. This invokes shame; wherever shame lives, worthlessness grows. It is important to separate the shadow emotions themselves, which should be embraced as latent energy waiting for you to use them positively, from the imbalanced, irresponsible, and hurtful reactions you sometimes choose and are what others react badly to in turn, which should be avoided at all costs.

Being on an inner trip, a spiritual path within, doesn't mean you will never feel insecure because your wife's new personal trainer, Giuseppe, is an Italian romance novel cover model, or become angry when your new boyfriend says he's actually not that into you. Negative feelings *will* come up, because they are fear-based and fear sometimes pops up unannounced. But remember: the shadow emotions don't define you. It's what you do with them that counts. Now and always, you can create yourself anew.

Now that you've demystified the shadows, embraced all the energy you contain, and stepped out into the light of awareness, let's have some fun creating a lifelong affair that you will enjoy and one that will never leave you wanting for love. As you go, keep in mind that loving yourself is like marriage: it's a choice and a daily, even hourly commitment you make to respect that promise, especially when it's the last thing you feel like doing. Don't abandon yourself by neglecting the gift of this affair because others have abandoned you or you've been hurt. Enduring heartache is the human condition; everyone goes through it. The question is, are you ready to move beyond waiting for someone else to soothe the pain inside, to learn to do it yourself? This is a radical step into your power, and though the experience of this level of independence is awesome, many people never try it. I want you to be the one who takes an oath, today, to begin a new phase of your inner relationship. Ask yourself, "What are your intentions with me?"

Then have a ceremony with some close friends and family where you will make a few vows that you will aim to never, ever break.

How to Jump-Start Your Affair—with Yourself

Ginga, in Brazilian Portugese, means "a sassy swing of the hips." It's how you walk when you've got confidence and life is good. It reminds me of another term, *joga bonito,* or "play beautiful." I first heard them both while watching a great documentary that followed a few teenage boys in Brazil as they tried out for professional soccer leagues. They were amazing, following a dream against all odds. *Ginga* gives you a clue about what attitude you must adopt if you, too, are going to play beautiful in this lifetime.

In the spirit of *ginga,* we'll stop being so serious now. Yes, you have a lot to think about. Yes, the road is hard at times, and yes, you will periodically need to take space and find a rest stop before someone is sorry. But actually living your own love affair requires that you become creative and have some fun. After all, in order to love you, you must first have some great times together!

Be Your Own Boyfriend or Girlfriend

Would you want to have a long-term relationship with someone who criticized you often, saying things like, "Hurry up! You're such a moron—I *knew* we'd be late," or "You look so fat in those pants. That's what you get for eating a pint of cookie dough ice cream last night. Take them off!" Or who lies on the couch every night in a bad mood, complaining about how bored he or she is, yet is too tired from working to do anything loving or interesting with you? Probably not.

That's why, when I was acting like that toward myself, I decided to change some things and make myself into my best boyfriend ever, because then I always have one to rely on. Because when I have a great loving relationship with myself, my fear and neediness is lessened, and outside relationships have less power over my self-esteem. Then, if I have a partner, it's an extra bonus—but it doesn't make or break my whole life.

How can you be someone you'd love dating? Create a Boyfriend/Girlfriend Wish List. Just write a few lines or keywords about the person you're looking for as a love partner. If you've already found one, lucky you; in this case, describe some of this person's qualities. Feel free to make a longer list, but don't go crazy. We're looking for a relationship attainable by two human beings, not illusory perfection. Perfection is a state where you always feel safe and never get challenged to improve or grow. How boring is that?

Steer away from describing physical attributes, and go for the heart. Instead of "Has buns of steel," try "Respects me and treats me as an equal."

Now take a good look at those words and honestly ask yourself: "Do I consistently treat *myself* this way?" Until you can answer yes, you can't truly give love or fully embrace it from others. So start doing these things for yourself.

It may be strange at first to be your own boyfriend or girlfriend if you're not used to it. And of course, it's excellent to choose—and enjoy—a partner who will do nice things to make your life easier. But you don't have to wait for someone else to start brightening your day. You can do it right now. I have an incredible significant other, and we love being together. Yet I love being by myself or with friends just as much. This kind of equality is something to emulate.

I will get you started. You can add to this list, too, but here are some situations where you might look to an outside source for help—but now you will see it's just as possible for you to handle these situations solo. When you can rescue yourself on bad days, you will free yourself every day from overasking it of others or looking to unhealthy sources to save you. Your loved ones will then surprise you by offering support, since they haven't been forced into it. Ask for assistance when you truly need it, but never demand that they take over for you. Freedom makes everyone free to give more.

You need: Help unwinding when you get tied up into the world's biggest ball of stress.

The usual: Call someone and complain, go have a few drinks, come home late, get into a needy fight with someone important to you because you're overwhelmed and now tipsy, and cry yourself to sleep.

Now you: When things get too heavy, it's time to lighten up! Instead of trying to figure everything out that's stressing you, take a clarity break. It's easy. Simply say to yourself, "Let's get out of here and . . ." And what? Watch a silly movie. Run a bath and give yourself a foot massage. Take it out on the exercise machine. Play a solo game of darts. Walk in the park barefoot. Go to a pet store (use caution or you might end up with a puppy). Any mindlessly fun activity will break the stress cycle and give you a fresh perspective on whatever you need to deal with next without getting more stressed or taking it out on those around you.

You need: Someone to listen to you when you've had the day from hell and need to vent, a person who actually seems interested and still loves you when the storm has passed.

The usual: Call your best friend, who had a bad day of her own. Vent. Get nowhere and frazzle you both. Call your husband at work. Vent. Get nowhere but more frazzled. Call your mother, who's on the phone with a frazzled Aunt Mary. Call others and reach only voice mail. Vent on tape. Cry with your forehead against the kitchen wall.

Now you: Get out of the house if possible, to a place that's calming, healing, and inspiring to you. Grab a notebook, a coaster, a napkin from the sushi joint, whatever. On a clean piece of paper, make two columns. On the left, write down: "All The Things That Sucked Today," then list everything you went through. On the right, write: "How This Can Eat My Dust."

To find some creative solutions, some of which should be silly and fun-loving, imagine that your closest friend just showed the left side of her list to you. How would you counsel him or her to deal with the situation? Sometimes, taking action is necessary; other times, all you can do is back off and give yourself a break while you wait for an answer to present itself.

All bad times, though, get better when someone wise who knows you best listens to you and gives you a new perspective. Find that one person, the one who always has your best interests in mind. Guess who that is? (Hint: Look in the mirror. Smile. Then wink. It's all you.)

Your *Me*-lationship

Now that you're being your own boyfriend or girlfriend, you can concentrate on your relationship between you and your soul. The quality of this interaction, at its best, will be a lifelong, meaningful partnership in which you will never be lacking for quality time, unconditional love, or heartfelt compliments.

This is the foundation for all experiences you will have with people, your job, and your whole outer world. If you are not putting the time and energy into this primary partnership, you will find that you are more easily knocked off your center when you start to involve yourself with other people. That's when your inner love affair, like any other, can become dysfunctional—when you neglect yourself too often in favor of making others happy. They don't get the best of you that way, and, even worse, neither do you. So, let's put this concept into action.

Make a list of five must-haves. These are nonnegotiable things you must have in any relationship so that you feel loved and appreciated. For example:

- Respect for the person you are and what you do
- Forgiveness of your mistakes and compassion when you struggle along your path

- A commitment to growing and deepening the relationship
- Regularly having quality time together
- A healthy and supportive attitude

Then, add a second column labeled "How I Can Give Them to Myself."

Use your imagination. When you learn to self-generate the things you need, you will begin to find that people who can't or won't give them to you begin to seem a lot less appealing. This simple action of loving yourself with a passion can also save a lot of heartache, power struggles, and wasted time. But you have to do it daily. To give you an idea of how to start, here are a few of my suggestions and the simple steps you can take to include your must-haves in your life:

- Acknowledgement that you are loved.
  How you can give it: Notes to yourself on the fridge, like "You're an amazing person, and I really love loving you!"

- Romantic gestures you get "just because."
  How you can give it: Your favorite flowers are waiting for you at the corner shop right now! You just have to go out and get them once a week.

- Feeling like you're sexy to someone besides yourself.
  How you can give it: Grab a fabulous male friend with excellent taste. Have him go clothes shopping with you. By the time you go out with him tonight, you'll be fabulous too!

Your list might be completely different from my suggestions, but you get the point. Once you've gotten to the root of self-attraction, you will naturally begin to broadcast the truly personal signal that your match will receive loud and clear, even if he or she is already around. You will be amazed at the response you will begin to receive from those who would be great partners, friends, and colleagues for you. Until then, and even then, keep circling this loving focus right back to you. This is where all the real work begins: each day, inside your heart. You're in the tunnel of love, and this ride seats only one.

Shadows into Light

How do you build your personal affair if you, like so many of us, have been engaging in a dysfunctional relationship with yourself? As in every love affair, it takes daily attention and constant communication. It takes doing something radically different to break the inner habit of criticism and begin standing up for yourself *to* yourself.

It also requires a healthy dose of creativity and commitment to make your solo time so exciting that you crave it when you haven't had enough. This is important: your love affair with yourself must not be boring, lonely, or something you do because you know you "should." Spending time with you can and must become one of the best parts of your day.

Let's learn how to lighten up some common shadow moments.

Faking It Till You Make It

What is faking it? It's a loving trick you play with yourself to jump-start your new affair. Sometimes you may not feel strong enough, brave enough, or interesting enough to maintain a whole inner relationship. Sometimes, however, changing your habits can come first—and then self-esteem will follow.

When you smile, even if you're not feeling amused, your brain reads the smile muscles and releases happy chemicals into your body. Taking actions that represent a strong sense of self end up making you truly feel that way. So faking it can become your reality sooner than you think. Maybe you're ready to take this step, and you don't need to fake it. Either way works.

Self-reliance is the point of this stop, so the next time you're waiting for the phone to ring and it doesn't, get up, get going, and do something empowering to turn your attention back to your own exciting life. Then when the phone *does* ring, it's a gift, not a lifeline. If it doesn't, who cares? You're out at the circus with your face painted like a tiger, laughing and eating cotton candy.

Independent people make preemptory strikes against emptiness all the time and keep themselves running on full. They
sometimes say, "I can't see you tonight, I'm working on my own
projects." It makes them much more interesting, because they
have a rich inner life to share.

Solo Date Night

When it comes to having a good time, you know what you need
better than anyone else does. Therefore, there is no excuse for having no fun.

Block out one night every week where you will take yourself
out for a date. It can be a lunch date, a dinner date, even a stay-
at-home date. Your date night will be sacred space, and no one
else gets to enter into it—not even if your new partner just got off
early from work and really wants to snuggle. Get a black permanent marker and write "Date with Self" on your calendar. Barring
an emergency, make this time as important as you would for a
hot date with Mr. or Ms. Right.

You hold this space not only to show yourself that you're
important, but to build a sense of self-reliance that allows you
to trust in your independence and ability to meet your world
one-on-one.

So how do you begin? Well, you know your likes and dislikes
better than I do. And you can absolutely go conventional—coffee
shops, parks, the library, and great movies are all lovely ways to
spend some quality time. Sometimes, however, a surprising date
night can become a memory you cherish. Being a little out of
the ordinary could become something you look forward to each
week. Why not spice things up? You deserve it.

On that note, here are two time-tested tools to help you start
creating zesty ideas for your solo nights out.

Pair-of-Dice Date Game

It's so fun, you'll think you just road-tripped to Vegas.

To play this game, you will need a pair of dice and the lists below of verbs and nouns. Use my ideas or write your own.

The Rules:

1. Roll one die for the verb (if you roll a 6, pick a verb from category 6).

2. Then roll the other die for the noun (if you roll a 4, pick a noun from category 4).

3. Match the verb and the noun together and violà—it's a road trip date!

4. No matter what, find a creative way to make the date happen within the next forty-eight hours.

Verbs:

1. Drive, eat, play, reclaim

2. Dress, flirt, find, sit

3. Draw, sing, drink, talk

4. Meet, watch, dance, make

5. Discover, photograph, buy, deliver

6. Take a swing at, write, join, create

Nouns:

1. North, east, south, west, more than ten miles away, some great place you read or heard about, any restaurant that requires a reservation, anywhere you stopped going because of *him* or *her*

2. Happy hour at a different bar, a coffeehouse with a notebook and a newspaper, the great American novel or its equivalent, this week's number one movie, your favorite food, a new hair/clothes/makeup look

3. A new friend, line-dancing, an unexpected gift, a cocktail named for you, the most attractive person in town,

"My Lips Are Sealed" by the Go-Gos or another favorite eighties song

4. Video games at the mall, the top ten songs on headphones at the record store, a hyped new artist's show, one sexy clothing item—and wear it, the dirtiest romance novel and the best chocolate you can find

5. Salsa dancing; bingo; a Stitch 'n' Bitch club or poker night; another state; a papier mâché piñata that looks like your boss, mother-in-law, or ex-boyfriend/girlfriend, even if only symbolically (donkeys are good for this)

6. An inspiring walk, a bookstore for your continuing education, grilled cheese sandwiches and diner-napkin poetry, your camera and a documentary attitude, someone else's high school reunion

Go Indie

Taking action to engage in your own interests instantly gives you strength and makes you more independent. Whether you're feeling like it or not, making a move toward your own dreams causes your life energy to expand and your heart to become more resilient to external fluctuations.

Write a list of your "Top Ten Indie Interests"—things you'd love to learn, work on, or create. What instrument do you want to play? Get a book and a guitar and start strumming. Is there a language you wish to learn? A masterpiece you'll finally begin? Or a set of macramé plant holders you've been dying to make? Something that needs sawing?

Hire a tutor, enroll in a college course, set aside time to do the projects and fun stuff that really make the time fly. You don't have to be a master at your craft—you just have to take the first steps toward your goals. With enough commitment, mastery will come, but it's really the process—where you feel like the artist you are, living out your passions—that counts most.

Leaving the Tunnel of Love

No matter what area of your life you wish to evolve, always start by getting your inner affair in order. Every day, choose words and actions, and say yes to only those things that bring a positive, expansive feeling to your heart. You always have this choice, so use it wisely and outrageously.

You can do this by setting aside, just for a few minutes, your focus on the responsibilities to anyone else in your life. Look deeply within and jump-start your new patterns by changing any dead-end behaviors you have and switching them for ones that promote the power of your true self.

If you can do this, you will never have to settle again. Then you may inspire those around you to step into their own integrity and self-respect in relating to themselves and to you. In a short time, your soul's echo will call to you the love you wished for all along—perhaps not knowing it was in you the whole time, only waiting for you to align with it.

No matter how you have been feeling, thinking, or acting, you can do things differently now, starting with the only person you can actually change—and your whole life will begin to re-create itself around your new behavior. In this way, we evolve and shift our experience of the world around us to reflect our hearts.

Congratulations! You've made it through the tunnel of love. Revisit often, re-create each day anew, and most important, have fun getting to know and love yourself.

the universal traffic light

The Art of Knowing When to Say No

The Wrong Way

I usually travel solo, because being on the road is a moving meditation for me—unless, of course, I hit New York City rush hour traffic, in which case it's more like a sitting meditation. But when I do invite someone else along, it's because I feel intuitively that the trip will be better served with this specific soul riding next to me. Turns out, I'm always right on about this—but I wasn't always.

Years ago, just before receiving the lesson of this stop, I was struggling mightily with my love relationship. My problem was that I was beginning to realize I wasn't with the right person for me, after two years of sharp and unpredictable emotional ups and downs, coupled with very little communication or positive growth in any aspect of the partnership. Since I was young and afraid of honest confrontations, my usual M.O. would be to start some drama and make the man think that his leaving me was his idea, rather than my passive-aggressive design. I never felt good about myself afterward, and my partners would usually not speak to me again. I instinctively felt there was some other way to communicate my needs, but I hadn't yet learned what it was.

In Max, I'd first come to see the value in having a man around at all times who could teach me how to fix the radiator on my 1969 AMC Rambler, or pick me up from work in mere minutes if the car stalled yet again in the parking lot. Plus, Max was cute and cool, and about two days out of every month we got along perfectly.

We fought often, mostly because I felt I couldn't trust him, and he would often prove me right. I wasn't happy, and it was getting worse. So after I announced that I needed to take a road trip to think over the status of our partnership and my place in it, Max demanded that I take him along, telling me it would be good for us to spend some time together, away from everyone. Although my ultimate goal wasn't to spend time with Max—it was to process my feelings about being with him—I said yes. I didn't want to argue anymore, and it seemed easier to agree to his demands than to face the struggle of saying no. Boy, was I wrong.

From the first mile, Max was already pointing out that he would be the navigator, since "as we all know, women can't find their way out of a paper bag," and changing my favorite jazz station to loud death metal. The trip was supposed to be two weeks long. It was—but *we* lasted three days.

The evening when Max remarked on the Cracker Barrel hostess and her great body—while she was still standing there—I knew he had to go. I'd been miserable during what should have been a powerful time of self-discovery and renewal. Instead, I'd been consumed with Max, his attitude, his wrongness for me, still placing his needs above mine.

So I asked for a time out. We stopped in a small town, and I went to a community park for a few hours, writing in my journal, discovering on paper what I'd known all along in my heart.

Over dinner, I calmly yet firmly laid it out for Max. I took full responsibility for my original agreement that he come along. I didn't blame him or get angry, but I did let him know that in this case, saying yes to him meant that I'd said no to my own happiness. I had to make a change, fast. I told him I'd decided not to be in the relationship anymore, and that my decision was final. I thanked him for the time and energy he'd spent on me and for the lessons I'd learned with him. I then offered to do what I could to help him in the transition out of the relationship. I said it all in exactly this many sentences. It didn't take many more for him to see that my mind was made up. Inside, I was freaking out, but I was finally ready to stand up for my future happiness.

Max was resentful, but he agreed to rent a car and drive back home. Once there, he'd decide what he needed to do to facilitate a separation from me. That was a lot to talk about at a restaurant, but sometimes these things can't wait.

On the day he left, I cried and mourned the good times we'd had. It was painful, but I knew I was back in alignment with my soul, and that gave me strength.

As I was driving out of town, I stopped at a traffic light. Another car pulled up next to me. The driver was a woman, and, at a glance, she looked a lot like me—red hair, sunglasses, fingers tapping to music. I remember thinking how random that my doppelgänger was just sitting right there. When my light turned green, hers somehow malfunctioned—strangest thing; as my light turned green, hers stayed red.

As I pulled away, I glanced over at her. She was looking at me with a bewildered expression, unable to go unless she pulled over into my lane, which she eventually did.

As I drove off, it hit me: I have two choices in any given moment, to say yes to my soul's signals and, like the green light, to move forward, or to say no, and remain stuck in negativity, stopped in my tracks at the red lights of life. One option will get me where I want to go and let me be freely *me*, the other will keep me idling, watching as others go speeding off toward their next adventure.

The Universal Traffic Light

This light is as big as the universe. It encompasses everything, including what you do, think, and feel. It is meant to guide you into staying on the road to your big yes. Unlike regular traffic lights, this one has no yellow. It shows only green or red because there is nothing in between saying yes or no. "Maybe" is an introspective limbo before you decide. It's okay to ponder and ruminate on an issue. For the sake of this stop, however, we're dealing with the moment when you make a decision.

The lights are really signals to keep you going with the flow of abundance. When you say yes to what is aligned with your soul, you'll get a green light. You will see openings and opportunities arise. You'll feel more peaceful, strong, hopeful, happy, creative, and excited to be alive.

When you say no to your soul's nature in any way, however, you'll trigger a red light. You will then see lanes of opportunity and doorways close off to you. You'll feel one or more of the emotional and physical symptoms of blocked life energy: fatigue, illness, sadness, depression, anger, fear, insecurity, and self-doubt.

The Big Yes

The big yes is an ultimate goal that guides your immediate behavior. It is a positive state of being, in which your actions come from intentions, beliefs, and emotions that serve your greatest good and help you realize your highest potential. To move toward your big yes in thought, word, and deed is to be more in alignment with love and to fuel your possibilities.

The big yes is made of multiple parts: your core values, what kind of person you wish to be, your life's work, and the things you love. When you're living in your big yes, the whole world benefits.

It is important to remember that you do not always have to say yes to get to your big yes. Sometimes you must to say no. This stop will teach you how to know the difference.

Because the big yes is your goal, any agreement or action you make now should serve it. If you do this more often than not, you will notice that your whole life will begin to harmonize, and abundance will flow back to you from every direction. The green light has blinked on, and it's a two-way light. Not only will you start moving ahead quickly, the whole universe will rush toward you as well, cocreating magic.

In yogic philosophy, we call the big yes your *dharma*. Dharma is a huge concept, an all-encompassing one that is also central to Buddhists and Taoists. On a universal level, it means to stand in true alignment and harmony with the ways of your soul and of nature. On an individual level, dharma entails doing what you were born to do and living as the whole person you are meant to be. When you are following your dharma, you are on the path, or *tao* of least resistance, and through this alignment with the flow of life, you become a more masterful creator of your reality. Dharma is your big yes, and you travel within your big yes by triggering as many green lights as possible and steering clear of the red ones.

To do this, you must concentrate on two actions:

1. Say yes to whatever gets you to your big yes.

2. Say no to what doesn't.

It sounds simple, and like any profound wisdom, it is. Mastering it into your life, however, takes practice.

Resistance

Technically, living your grandest dreams and doing what makes you feel good should be easy. So why are many people still not doing it? They are stuck in jobs they hate, relationships that aren't right, daily grinds that are wearing them out. They look around to find that life has become mediocre at best, and they're nowhere close to where they thought they'd be by now.

Any change, even the most positive, is deeply terrifying. Remember, at a deeply unconscious level your mind thinks, "If I'm not dead right now, I'm safe. I can't do anything differently, or I might die." It's a basic survival instinct that might keep us from walking off a cliff, but listening to it won't get us the life we deserve. We have an instinctual aversion to moving in any direction, especially to the next level, which is as yet unknown.

Add to this our fears that we're not good enough to live our big yes, that if we fail we'll have nothing to live for. We listen to people around us think our dreams are unrealistic. We're afraid they're right. Top off this fraidy-cat cocktail with a lot of confusion about where to go from here, and we've created the master controller of all our red lights: resistance.

Resistance happens any time we stand in the way of our own forward momentum. We block ourselves from real happiness, love, and fulfillment in countless ways. There are the obvious ones, such as self-doubt, but also the more covert, including procrastinating, rationalizing, and engaging in drama. Resistance is a destroyer of dreams. Yet it is also completely in our power to triumph over it. And we must weaken its power over us, or it will paralyze us from attaining our big yes.

When you're busy doing what you don't like, acting in ways you're not proud of, and erecting imaginary roadblocks to your future, it keeps you from everything you want. History is haunted by the ghosts of books that should have been written but weren't; soul mates who never got up the courage to say, "I love you"; and inventions, businesses, and masterpieces that could have served humanity but never reached the drawing board. Anytime you let internal or external resistance stop you from doing and being with love, you have made the choice to allow the red light onto your path. You need to take measures to keep it out. For example, you might have lost your job, but you can write one page a day and then submit the material to agents in your spare time, right? See your big yes globally, then act locally. Unlike the choice between yes and no, this isn't all or nothing, but a process of moving unerringly toward your goals in steps, and every day. Even a little movement toward your big yes counts, big time.

When you come upon resistance in your life, rejoice. That's right—celebrate! When it appears, you can be pretty sure that you're heading in the direction of your big yes. In a glorious book on resistance, *The War of Art*, author Stephen Pressfield explains, "Like a magnetized needle floating on a surface of oil, Resistance will unfailingly point to true North—that calling or action it most wants to stop us from doing. We can use this. We can use it as a compass. We can navigate by Resistance, letting it guide us to that calling or action we must follow before all others."

Instead of pushing resistance away, which is more resistance, use it to orient you to the direction of abundance. You do this by learning how to say yes and no properly. Most people know how to say these words, yet they use them backward, and unwittingly create a big red light. Let me show you what I mean.

Saying Yes

There are two ways to use the word *yes*. One will get you where you want to go and the other will keep you waiting forever.

The first is the more common, yet ineffective, *over yes*. We could call it the "oy," because that's what you say when you realize you've done it. Over-yessing is what occurs any time you've agreed to do something that drains you or diverts your energy away from your big yes. When a neighbor asks you to watch her kids, and you say yes even though you're exhausted and she could get someone else? Oy. It is not balanced or inherently spiritual to give so much that you have nothing left for yourself. That kind of yes tells the universe that you are someone who is willing to be depleted, that you'll say okay to anything, even if it's to your detriment. By such actions, you'll attract more people who will ask you for big favors, pile up too much work, give you less free time, and leave you a whole lot more resentful. Plus, by taking over for someone, you take away an opportunity for those who need help to self-generate it or get it from someone who actually wants to give it.

The over yes is actually a form of resistance, as is anything that reroutes you from your ultimate goals. It comes in many packages: you say it by allowing obsessiveness, worrying, perpetuating anxiety, overthinking everything, as well as by taking action when you don't have to. You've been to the gas station, and you know how to balance your life energy. Now add the awareness that, just maybe, you might be choosing to remain in an overgiving state because it gives you a reason not to try what scares you.

It's beautiful to offer assistance and to give because another is in need. But make sure that you're consistently doing your own work. Then, once in a while, if a need is worthy, give something that you can spare, and keep enough for yourself.

The second way to use the affirmative is to master the *intelligent yes*. This is something you agree to do, think, or say, that will serve your big yes.

When you receive an opportunity that seems to green-light your heart, be it an invitation, a job, a friend, or anything else—if it makes you feel happy, say yes. Say yes even if you're scared. I always say that happy fear means you're taking the risk to really live. Congratulations!

I've come across people who stubbornly cling to the illusion of an artist: that to do anything outside their "life's work" is unacceptable, so they refuse to get another type of job, even when they need money to buy art supplies or a home in which to paint. As a result, they remain caught in the web of resistance, with no income, no reliable living space, and therefore, no life's work. Be aware that you may sometimes need to do things you don't love to pave the way for your most excellent future. Being stuck for years in a dead-end job is not an intelligent yes. Working for one year in a great-paying job that you're not passionate about, to make enough money to put yourself through a master's program in your dream field? Smart.

Look at your life now. Where have you been oy-ing, and where could you reorient toward more intelligent uses of your time and energy?

Saying No

How you say no can be just as helpful—or destructive—toward your dharma as a yes.

There are two types of no: the *over no*, and the *intelligent no*. Just as an over yes is an energy drain caused by giving away too much positive energy, the over no drains you with negative energy. It happens whenever you become destructive, reactive, critical, judgemental, blaming, yelling, or otherwise nasty when attempting to set your boundaries. The problem with the over no is that it depletes your life force, and you have very little left over to do any good work within the boundary you set. The over no is so messy we could call it the oh-no! because that's what we feel like after we act with disregard for ourselves and others.

Most people think the over no is the only way they can decline to participate in or disagree with things. It takes many forms. There's the personal over no, when you berate yourself or feel guilty for what you don't like about yourself. The interpersonal over no is when you let anger and defensiveness get the better of you with others, causing fights, drama, and unnecessary grief. The worldwide over no finds you railing against society, other countries, the president, poverty, and any other big external issues that you "hate." There are problems in the world, people who act like jerks, things about yourself to shift, times you need to stand your ground and say no, but you're not going to make a positive difference by being as negative as the very things with which you disagree. And it certainly doesn't feel very good or get you any closer to your big yes. In fact, it keeps you far from it.

Here's where the intelligent no comes in—a highly underused skill that if applied even part-time could keep you in green lights forever. Saying no with awareness and foresight takes knowing when and how to decline to use your life energy toward any given situation. If the intelligent yes is what to do toward your big yes, the intelligent no is what *not* to do to get closer to it.

One major thing you don't want to do is stunt your positive growth. Also, you should avoid bringing more vibrations of anger and disagreement into the world. There is a way to make sure that you don't add to a problem, just because you want it to change.

It might surprise you to learn that one of the two best ways to get to your big yes is to say no. Yet saying no is often neglected, since setting positive boundaries is uncomfortable for many open-hearted people. It's hard to decline to help, or to contain yourself when you really want to scream at someone. Mastering the no, however, is the other half of a holistic spiritual practice.

What would you like better: a baseball thrown so hard and thoughtlessly it hits your head, or a ball tossed more mindfully, with the respect of a teammate, so you can catch it? Similarly, you'll get a better response if you gently toss something back, rather then hurling it at someone, hard.

The hard throw is violent, disrespectful, and divisive: it makes one person seem in control, and the other is at that person's mercy. It's seizing power that should not belong to you and the interaction becomes a dictatorship. The soft throw makes the exchange a partnership: even if the person doesn't want to catch the ball, he or she at least was given the respectful choice. This is the mark of equality. Now the ball is in the other person's court. You've done your job by lobbing it back their way, and the person must make his or her own decision how to handle it from there.

There is an African proverb famously repeated by Theodore Roosevelt that says, "Speak softly and carry a big stick; you will go far." When you carry the "big stick" of remaining in your big yes, you do not have to attack or defend by using over nos. You can state a refusal quietly, with respect, and still stand strong in the knowledge that your decision is what your soul needs to do, be, or say.

This is the difference between the over no and the intelligent one. The first will only create more anger, separation, and distance. With the second, people might still not like your decision, but at least you will be acting from a place of unity and compassion, and so you can move forward positively, knowing that you haven't tried to hurt or divide anyone.

When you use an intelligent no, you are finding a way to decline to participate in something that would create a detour to your big yes, and you will avoid as much negative energy as possible in the process. You will soon learn how to transform every "Hell, no" into a "No, thank you."

Don't Be Sneaky

Sometimes we sound respectful, or we use our yes and no to get what we want, but on the inside, we're still doing it out of a fear-based, separatist place. If you say to your husband's sister, "Sorry, Mary, Bob and I can't have dinner with you as planned," but you're doing it because you're secretly jealous of their close bond, then you haven't taken action from the most harmonious place.

Whenever you use your actions to manipulate a situation to your seeming advantage, or to keep people apart instead of promoting unity, you are still going to keep attracting separation and fear. You can't hide from the universe, even on the inside. So have courage and stand up for what you know you really need, whatever the outcome might be. Your yes and no needs to not only sound loving but be loving.

The Yoga of Yes and No

Choosing to act only in accordance with your big yes, whether you have to employ an intelligent yes or no to do that, has its roots in ancient yoga philosophy. Patanjali is a man who researchers believe lived sometime between 100 and 500 BC, yet he remains one of the guiding sages for modern life. He wrote the Yoga Sutras, a compilation of short aphorisms that encourages readers to keep their state of mind, body, and heart always in service to their highest self. Pantanjali discusses the *yamas*, or how to cultivate energetic self-control even in the most challenging of times. The *yamas* describe how we can interact with the world at large from this place of inner discipline. *Yama* is literally translated as "restraint," and this one little word can unlock vast amounts of life force. As a spiritual practitioner interested in honing your vision, you must understand and practice restraint. You must know when to act and also when *not to act*. This balance creates a wholeness of heart and spirit and helps you define yourself instead of scattering to the winds. Two of the *yamas* in particular that help to govern this stop are *ahimsa* and *Brahmacharya*.

Ahimsa, or nonviolence, is the main principle by which Gandhi lived. Although it asks us not to do the obvious forms of harm, like killing people, this principle also invites us to consciously choose our words and deeds so that they do the least amount of damage. This includes the damage done to yourself, so in any relationship, even if you have to cause pain, you need to try not to do it in a destructive way. Even when facing the most rude, thoughtless comment or imbalanced person, you can still be considerate of everyone involved. You'll do so not necessarily because you feel they deserve good treatment, but because you know that to speak in misalignment with your values is to diminish your energy vibration to that of a negative person's.

Road Rule

When confronted with lower vibrations, don't lower yourself—raise yourself higher!

Acting in dissonance with how you really want to be hurts you, by running poisonous energy through your body, mind, and heart. This behavior is one aspect of the saying, "What you do to others, you also do to yourself." It violates the principle of ahimsa: harming yourself to please another, hurting someone unnecessarily by being careless, or hurting someone on purpose by acting defensively, manipulatively, or just plain badly. If you find yourself about to choose one of these behaviors, practice restraint. Keep quiet, and then reflect through your heart until you can say what you must with clarity, respect, and nonharm.

Then there's the concept of Brahmacharya. Historically, people thought this term meant "to be celibate," or "to retain sexual energy." After studying it in depth, I believe it to be a much more refined concept than that. If you break down the word, *Brahma* describes ultimate reality, which is bliss and knowledge, your biggest yes of all. *Char* means "to follow or practice." So to practice Brahmacharya is to lead your life in a way that is always honoring and keeping in mind your big, blissful yes. To do this, you must start containing your energetic leaks and stop expending your energy in ways that do not maintain your ultimate state of being.

In contemporary terms, this ancient principle can guide you to make more intelligent decisions about what to do with your actions: Do you need to give out, or do you need to keep something now to serve your greater good and, therefore, that of those around you?

Aligning with peace and love might sound like a retro hippie ideal, but in fact it's the only thing you can ever do to effect change. And sometimes, you have to set major boundaries to become an ambassador for the power of positivity.

A perfect example of this is Gandhi. He saw how the British colonization of India was hurting and demeaning his countrymen. He saw military force used to kill his people and knew he was up against the government and army of an entire nation. Yet to manifest his opposition to violence and disempowerment, he did not fight back in the same negative way, by amassing an army of his own and starting a war, or by pushing against what he didn't want from a fear-based place of anger and force. He realized that reacting this way would actually be agreeing with their methods by stooping to mimic them.

Instead, Gandhi used an intelligent action: he turned and walked hundreds of miles to the ocean, picking up thousands of supporters along the way. He asked his followers to make their own salt from the sea, since the government had put a tax on salt and a ban on this activity. The administration tried to stop this, along with the grassroots industry of the homespun clothes Gandhi encouraged everyone to make, the hunger strikes, the nonviolent peace marches. Gandhi peacefully went to jail multiple times and used those periods behind bars to continue writing and speaking of independence and equality for his countrymen. The positive force of his masses could not be stopped, and eventually the British realized they could not remain in power. Their imperial command was swept away by the true strength of loving action and unmovable conscious boundaries.

This one man set forth such soft and powerful nos that in his lifetime, his nonviolent revolution was victorious. Gandhi accomplished all of this by doing the *opposite* of those things he disagreed with—war, force, occupation, disempowerment, fear. In terms of his life and those of millions affected by him, he *became* his big yes—through nonharming, power through knowledge, integrity, self-sufficiency, simplicity, and courage. By acting intelligently upon his vision, he became a beacon, attracting a great community of like-minded people, and together they made a huge difference. Still he continued, teaching these principles to others, through his personal thoughts, words, and deeds. He did what most people thought impossible—all without straying from his soul's values.

Through his living example, Gandhi taught us the way to transform any situation we don't want in our life and our world one life at a time, starting with your life, right now. With more and more of the world waking up to their true potential and knowing that, as Gandhi demonstrated, the positive force is infinitely more powerful than the negative, even one person acting from his or her big yes can change the world.

Remember that there is *never* a time when screaming no at someone or something will affect a positive change. Only positive energy can attract a positive outcome—it's the universal way.

take the wheel
Find Your Big Yes

To figure out your big yes, write down those qualities that you most admire in the people who have inspired you. Then write down your strengths and talents, and list as well the things that you're passionate about doing and creating. Write a paragraph about the kind of life you think would be a perfect match for you. What would you be doing? With whom? Pay attention to the people, places and experiences that have made you feel at home in your skin. Which ones do you feel negative around or in disharmony with? Write those down, too.

Look at your words now. Think about the person you want to be and what kind of legacy you wish to leave your loved ones.

Now take all you've written and condense it down to one short paragraph, beginning with, "The kind of life I intend to have is . . ." The shorter the better: as you've learned, the most profound truths can be said in very few words.

Writing this paragraph is the first step in determining your big yes, and although you should refine it over time, you now have a guide to everything you intend, think, feel, create, speak, and do. If an action or an idea doesn't match your soul's mission statement, don't do it, say it, or continue thinking it.

Intelligent No-ing

Before saying yes, you'll learn to respectfully conserve your energy, so you will have some to redirect toward your goals. You'll do this by using an intelligent no.

Anytime you need to set a boundary, speak your mind about something you disagree with, or otherwise decline an offer or invitation, you might begin with one of the following statements. Continue the list on your own, too, in the language of respect that would work in your world.

- Oh, sorry—I can't right now. If I can later, do you want me to let you know?
- I would if I could, but I've got a prior engagement then.
- I have to be honest: I'm feeling really drained, and I need to recharge before I make any more commitments.
- I'm feeling [insecure, agitated, frustrated] about this right now. I don't want to get reactive, so I think I'll take a little space [a thirty-minute walk, an hour by myself, a night off], and I'll call you when I feel more centered.
- I'm not so into this. I think I'll take a cab home. I'll see you later.
- That's not something I'm comfortable doing. How about this instead?
- I'll have to decline your invitation. But thank you for thinking of me!
- I've already promised my time to others. Can we plan something in the future? [If you're not interested in a future date, say only the first sentence.]
- Oh, wow, that's a great idea. But I'm already maxed out. What about Jean? I know she's [good at/interested in/a possible resource for] your project! [People love to be referred to another option if you're unavailable.]
- No, but thanks for asking.

Bite-Size Your Big Yes

In a culture that loves to supersize things, you could find yourself overwhelmed if you think of your big yes as something you have to do all of, all at once all the time. Don't let the bigger picture loom so large that you don't know where to start, and so you never do. Instead, bite-size your major goals into smaller actions that you can take, starting today.

Write down some of your future goals for yourself, for example: "I want to live by an ocean." Then, under each goal, brainstorm things you can do to move yourself closer to it. These actions will be intelligent yeses and nos that you will use to align yourself with what you want to achieve most of all. Some you can do in five minutes, like "Put a picture of the perfect beach house in my office." Others might take a little time, like researching jobs in beach communities, so bite-size them further, and say, "Friday mornings, I will spend one hour e-mailing friends to ask about their favorite places, and researching online," then "I will save $50 per week toward a trip to the area that interests me most," then, "This week I will send my résumé out to the contacts from the lovely community I found." When you take small actions consistently enough, they add up to make a big difference.

Change Your Light Meditation

Whenever you feel challenged, or stuck around communication with another person, reflect on these suggestions for transforming any situation from negative (red light) to positive (green light). Write down all the places or interactions in your life where you need to make a switch. Think about how you would like other people to communicate the same issue to you, if the situation were reversed. Use the exact same words with them. Or in the words of another sage, "Do unto others as you would have them do unto you." Then, no matter how they choose to respond, you've come from your best intentions. Stay nonreactive and firm.

Road Rule

Integrity is a two-way street. If you wouldn't put up with it, don't dish it out.

The situation: You're stressed because your boss is constantly critical of your work, and when he tells you about it, he's not respectful.

Your big yes: To feel competent at your job and be appreciated for the good work you do; to live a less stressful life.

You could: Constantly complain about how bad it is at work, change nothing, drink five shots to numb the stress each night before bed. One day, you can't take it anymore. You march into your boss's office the morning of the big proposal you've promised to him and say, "You know what, buddy? I've had enough of your disrespect. I'm outta here. I quit!" It might feel freeing in the moment to tell him off, but in the end, you'll gain a reputation for being unreliable and volatile—not so good for your greater goal of getting a better job with nicer people. Plus, if you look closely, you'll see that you just acted with the same attitude—disrespect— that you are telling the universe you don't want to accept into your life. You can't have it both ways.

Make the switch: Ask yourself: Is the criticism valid? Then look at where you might be falling short and take steps to improve those places. Are you always late? Be on time. If you're doing your best, and it's your boss's personality that's negative, start looking for another opening managed by someone who will value you more. You will be surprised at the offers you'll get if you approach the situation in a positive manner. In the meantime, ask supportive co-workers for their feedback so you feel some appreciation. And while you're at it, do some yoga—and lay off the alcohol. Look away from the red light in every way as you move toward your big yes with every action.

The situation: Your partner comes home from work tired and is unable to relate as well as he or she usually can. He or she needs time alone, or at least easy quiet for about two hours. This scenario doesn't work for you; it's a time when you'd prefer to reconnect since you don't see each other all day long. You, understandably, don't like the feeling of distance each evening at five, and your partner, understandably, has little to give. Yet the two of you argue about it often. You can't understand why your partner can't be more affection- ate even if he or she is tired. You would be!

The big yes: To feel an emotional connection with your part- ner; to know that you're important to the mate you've cho- sen and to be existing in a state of mutual appreciation and respect.

You could: Get upset the moment your partner walks in the door and isn't as loving as usual. Become critical and blam- ing. Your mate withdraws further, becoming more sullen and silent, and eventually leaves the room to escape and get what he needs: space. You stop seeing what this per- son does well and instead are hyperfocused on his short- comings. You use a hard no, just to put the icing on the cake: turn on him at the dinner table, after getting short answers to your questions, and yell, "Fine! Have your space! You never give an inch of connection when *I* need it!" before storming into the bathroom and crying. Your partner, who simply needed time to regroup, feels trapped, guilty, and more exhausted than when he walked in. The entire night is uncomfortable, and no one gets a resolution.

Make the switch: You want to feel connected and to fulfill your own needs, but you're in a partnership, so the trick is to see further—to understand what your partner needs in order to be able to give you what you need back. In this case, your partner asked for some decompression time before he can give anything to anyone else. Most evenings, when your partner arrives home, be either just leaving for a couple of hours with your friends, taking the kids for a long walk, talking on the phone with someone you love, or engrossed in a movie or a project you scheduled specifically for the two hours (or one hour, or thirty minutes) that your partner seems to need to segue back into his or her relationship frame of mind. If you work as well, make some interesting plans a few times a week that will keep you otherwise focused after work for the necessary decompression period.

You're not playing a game—you are giving yourself what youneed: connection, caring, and fun. You do this because you realize you are never going to get it from your partner right when he or she can't give it; using an over no and then becoming upset at the person for not doing what you want is not the answer.

Instead, let your partner know your plan, without blame, because you know some time to

> *It is well to give when asked, but it is better to give unasked, through understanding.*
>
> —KAHLIL GIBRAN

transition is required and you want to support that process. And since, after a long day, your relaxation style is to connect and share with friends and loved ones, you're going to do it in a way that you hope will work for both of you. Just say that. Nicely. Now you've offered your mate something out of understanding and caring that he or she is asking for, while you simultaneously say yes to what you want. Then watch how your partner, without one ounce of nagging, transforms into someone who is much more willing and able to smother you with affection *when you come back together.*

If you're going to yell at someone to "respect my needs," then you sure better be willing to do the same for them first.

The situation: You're upset about a family drama.

Make the switch: Be firm and clear with your family that you will no longer give energy toward or discuss pointless bickering but are happy to listen and support any solution-oriented direction they want to undertake. Then do it. Respond only to actions and people who are balanced and healthy. Make sure you don't carry the drama over into your other relationships.

The situation: You're horribly stressed about your mounting debt.

Make the switch: Sit down with a debt counselor and figure out a rational repayment plan. Brainstorm with a financially minded friend or a financial coach and see what you can do about thinking, feeling, and acting wealthier on the inside and outside, than you have been. (See Stop #8, the Treasure Cove, for examples.)

The situation: You're sick of the current president.

Make the switch: Vote for someone else, and while you're at it, vote for federal and local candidates who actively represent your political views. Donate to your favorite causes. Or run for office yourself!

The situation: You're angry because children of the world are going hungry.

Make the switch: Check out www.ChildrenInternational.org or similar initiatives. For just $22 a month, you can make a difference. Visit www.freerice.com. At no cost to you, rice is donated to starving families.

Well, what are you waiting for? Do something, anything to make an intelligent switch in whatever areas are bothering you, right now. Then repeat the new behavior tomorrow, too. Through doing, you'll see that you can make a difference, at the very least in your own heart, and you'll gain the courage to do more. The relationships in question will have to transform, because you did. If they don't change enough to fulfill you, then you have another choice to make. But regardless, you'll be in a much improved inner state as you decide.

Forty Days of Yes

As known by ancient masters and contemporary psychologists alike, changing habits is hard but possible. You must repeat the new behavior for a period of time before it will really stick.

It takes just over a month to fully get into your brain, change the old habit, and make the transformation strong. Many traditions suggest forty days as the perfect span. We'll use this latter model to conduct an experiment. This process is designed to get you into the habit of seeing, feeling, and acting from a positive place of abundance, so you will not only literally change your mind about your life, but you will also see your life change to match your mind, as you take different actions from your different intentions.

Intention initiates the process. For these forty days, your mantra will be: "I will live only from my big yes, saying yes to what serves it and no to what doesn't." For the next forty days, turn only toward love, creativity, respectful boundaries, adventure—all that you want more of in your life. You will simultaneously turn your attention away from negativity and resistance wherever you find it. If something feels bad, find a way to feel good. If you don't want to do something, think of an inspired way to decline.

To stay on track, you will check your emotional and mental state throughout the day. If you start feeling, thinking, or acting stressed out, angry, frustrated, judgmental, critical, or controlling, you'll know you're backsliding into the habit of your big no and all the negative, resistant beliefs you hold. The longer you stay in the no state, the more red lights you'll turn on. No matter what you want to change or you don't like, you must switch to viewing it from a big yes perspective, or resistance will grow brighter.

To get into a big yes mindframe, each day, whenever possible, think, feel, and do mostly what you align with and feel good about. For example, instead of:

- Gossiping about people
- Engaging in drama
- Talking about all your health, job, or relationship problems
- Stressing over bills, responsibilities, or other things
- Criticizing or getting upset at your mate/children/yourself
- Practicing your various resistance techniques

you'll do this:

- Speak only highly of people or, if you don't think highly of them, think less about them. And don't talk about anyone—not even the latest scandal-plagued celebrity—over the water cooler. What if she was your child? Would you still think the comments were acceptable?

- Disengage from drama. Politely get off the phone, refuse to participate further in destructive choices (yours or other people's), and leave the situation until you and the other parties people can deal in solutions and caring support.

- Talk about the good things in your life: aspects of your health, job, or relationships that are working. As for the rest, communicate only in positive facts. Instead of talking about how much you hate your job, and thereby energizing feelings of your hating your job, try this: "My work isn't my ultimate career, but I'm learning valuable things that will help me as I move toward my full potential."Let the medical professionals deal with your health if you're ill, then stay in a healing mentality. Don't talk with your friends about how awful your mate is—or vice versa. Focus on other people's good qualities, and if there are challenges, speak of solutions with compassion. Keep an open heart and decide what's best for you from there.

- Do what you can about your bills, take on only as much responsibility as you can handle and still stay balanced, and then find ways to be in inner abundance so outer abundance can find you.

- Compliment your mate/children/yourself for what they're doing that's positive. Ask kindly for what you need, with respect and in the spirit of partnering with equals. But above all, acknowledge the qualities of your loved ones that are working for you. Tell them what they do that helps you feel welcome, happy, and loved. If you need to express displeasure, only and always, do it with the same respect you'd ask for yourself.

It Isn't Easy Being Green

At first, the forty days will be intense. You'll have to focus more during this time to get the same results that will come easier later on. Habits are hard to break—in the beginning. But once you practice this new way, and things start working better in your world, your new habit will become a joy and a pleasure.

Ask more of yourself. Sit with the discomfort of containing your reactivity and anger until you can alchemize it into intelligent action. Align with your best intentions and watch the negativity begin to dissolve from all areas of your life.

If at any time you find yourself in a situation where you cannot seem to get past an obstacle of negativity, remove yourself from the dynamic immediately and go do something you love, until you are back in a place of clear seeing. Actions taken from this place will serve everyone better. Whenever you falter, as we all must do to learn and strengthen our practice, do what it takes to get back on track.

As you practice the art of switching red lights to green, as with any skill, you will get better at seeing the signals as you go and will be able to navigate your desired road more quickly. Now that you're picking up speed, let me be the first to welcome you to the fast lane!

the carpool lane

Deciding Who Gets a Ride and Who Eats Your Dust

my trip
A Graduate Degree in Life

Right after graduating from college in Seattle, I found myself with two degrees and no direction. After university, watching as most of my college friends scattered to the four winds of their futures, I had no idea which way to go or how to put my bachelor's degrees in journalism and sixteenth-century French literature to any realistic use.

I needed to get onto the open road and hear myself think. I knew if I could get some space around me, with enough hyperactive brain cells lulled quiet by the passing gravel, I would surely receive a road-trip inspiration about the next step.

Why I decided, at the last minute, to look on the "Ride Needed" board at the student union and invite three complete strangers along for the trip is beyond me. I think it had something to do with being too young to know better, feeling the first stirrings of altruism, and probably also with the seductive allure of gas money.

On the morning of our departure, I met my three car mates for the first time. They would share a major part of my trip as I dropped them off at their hometown destinations and would also pay for most of the drive. It seemed like a pretty good deal to me—until they arrived.

Bullet was a tough punk from L.A. She had bright red dreadlocks down to her waist, with actual bullet casings woven in. She wore combat boots about two years before they came into style, and after she shook my hand, it hurt until the next day. Steve was athletic—loved football and baseball and, as I later found out, lots and lots of beer. He was headed to Astoria, Oregon, to see his brothers. My final passenger, Mindy, was a beautiful blond wispy girl who was going to San Francisco to try out for a ballet company. She seemed so vulnerable and sweet, like a baby deer.

I had no idea how these very different people would get along in a confined space for a few hours. All I knew was that my gas was being paid for—how bad could it get? Well, Steve started a bar brawl with an entire country-western band, and we had to wait five hours to collect him from the police station. He didn't like them playing "Achy Breaky Heart," apparently. Mindy wouldn't eat anything, and she had four low-blood-sugar attacks, fainting once in line at a fast-food restaurant, and we waited three hours for her to be released from the hospital. Then Steve broke up with his girlfriend (loudly) on a pay phone while we were stopped to get gas (a two-hour wait). Then Mindy felt anxious and made us drive to an electronics store so she could find a white-noise machine that plugged into the cigarette lighter so she could meditate in the car. The store didn't sell them, so everyone had to be quiet for an hour while she chanted "*Om mani padme hum*" about a thousand times. Throughout the whole thing, Bullet was helpful where help was needed, yet eerily silent. I wondered when she'd snap too and I'd find out how far she'd go over to the Dark Side.

Needless to say, for the entire trip, between Mindy and Steve, I did nothing but damage control. The drama was constant, and my quiet, inspirational trip was out the window. All I knew was that I had to get these people out of my car, forever. As I dropped Steve off, then Mindy, I felt a palpable clearing around me. Even though Bullet remained for a couple more hours, I felt good and happy and began a conversation with her that, to my total surprise, sparked a lifelong friendship. She delighted me with her witty side, her knowledge of fashion and literature, and the spiritual side that urged her to wear the uniform of a fighter, so when people inevitably asked her about it, she could openly share her passion for peace.

Bullet, or Shannon, as she answers to these days, went on to start her own theater company where she produces meaningful works by new playwrights. We're on the West and East coasts, but we talk regularly on the phone, supporting each other through thick and thin, men and jobs and big decisions. Who knew that out of those three passengers, the one who seemed most different from me on the outside would turn out to be a true soul sister within?

the map
Pick Your Pool

Now that you've achieved so much inner knowledge and begun to increase your speed, you can turn your attention toward your carpool: all your outer relationships. As you've seen from my stories, and perhaps as you've lived in your own, inviting the wrong person along for the ride can ruin a perfectly good adventure. The people with whom you choose to spend the majority of your time will color your experience of life.

Your carpool comprises everyone you relate to who affects you emotionally in some way. There are different levels of your carpool, however, based on how close each person is to your heart. Think of it as concentric circles widening from a central point. That point, of course, is you, and closest to you are those whom you trust the most, such as your love partner, some family, and friends. Then you expand to include people you care about but may keep at a little more distance for various reasons. Then we have acquaintances and necessary people, such as co-workers or your boss's wife. Farther out are those you hold at a great arm's length, and you may or may not see them much, or want to. Even if you are keeping any kind of boundary up with someone, you are still in a relationship.

Each person in your life should be relegated to the appropriate circle and held to the standards of that placement. Many people are polar with their relationships: either they let too few into their most intimate space, or they let in anyone who comes along. Also, they put people in the wrong areas and allow themselves to be hurt by becoming too open, too intimate with others who are not capable of that level of emotional health, or shut out those who would be good to have closer. It's important to differentiate between the nuances of each circle and set your boundaries accordingly. Not everyone should get to know your most vulnerable self. That honor is reserved for those who have shown you that you can open to them safely. Yet it is also necessary to be open to possibilities, to know that people can change and that you can trust more of them more often than you might think.

When it comes to other people, mastering the skill of carpool creation is a valuable tool for living a joyous life. Try as you might, if you surround yourself with negative people, it will be infinitely more challenging for you to get your soul's work done. Ultimately, those you keep around deeply affect your inner road trip. To clear your way toward becoming the best of yourself, it's in your interests to relate most often to friends, family, partners, and co-workers who bring out the best in you, not the worst.

To know how to make a powerful carpool, you must practice the spiritual principle of *viveka*, or discernment, which is the act or process of exhibiting keen insight and good judgment. It's also the trait of judging wisely and objectively. Discernment is the art of deciding, of making conscious choices. Knowing who you are is the first step, and then you decide where you need boundaries and where you should stay open to enliven your soul. The highest form of discernment is to know that what you are choosing will add to your big yes, rather than take away from it, then making each decision for exactly that reason.

To be successful and fulfilled on any level you must: know in your heart what you want, decide upon attaining it, and go to great lengths to get it. While you do this, I want you to have the kind of people around you who light your fire, and not settle for anything less. We live in a culture of settling, and also one of deep dissatisfaction—they are inextricably linked.

Discernment helps you set limits in some places and reach out in others, to create a healthy balance of nourishing relation-ships to counter the ones we must all temporarily deal with that aren't so great.

There are some people, such as your superiors at work, whom you may not like personally, but professionally they help you get to your ultimate goal. That's okay. Just be careful that you are not expecting your boss to be, say, a father figure to you, and when he turns out not to be one, you get hurt and upset. If, through dis-cernment, we can place those we know into their proper arenas, we will be able to release our false expectations of them, and much heartache begins to clear. People can cross circles and become bet-ter friends, or more distant ones. But who they are in the moment will determine where they reside in your carpool. Discernment is most powerful when you keep the past in mind, then you look at what's happening right now, and let that direct your choices.

If you don't yet have people around who really excite you—a lover, the great friends—don't worry. As you decide who you're going to be and use *viveka* to act in accordance with your big yes, you'll gravitate toward yourself more like-minded people. You could also call this your "tribe"—those who get you who may not be the same as you but fully appreciate who you are. Since you've built more confidence and self-esteem over the course of your road-trip, you will now accept more of this. You will no longer be as affected by those who seek to diminish you, and you'll become less interested in replaying old dramas. You know better, so you will choose better. When all of this happens enough, you will look around yourself and see that your world has changed. All you can do is make a work of art of your internal revelations and external actions—and that will give you far more positive options to choose from.

Just as you can't create other people's lives, they can't make you change into anything you don't want to be—only if you choose to feel or act a certain way will you shift. Yet they can affect you, as you affect them. In this way, people can be a source of healing and love or dysfunction and stress. You can do all the work in the world on yourself, but if you surround yourself with people who bring you down, you're probably not going to be as successful as you could be, or at least you'll have to work much harder to succeed, than if you'd gathered around you a supportive, positive community. Why waste your time and vitality when your ride could be much smoother and the company so much more fun?

The Carpool Lane

It's just another form of resistance to engage in struggles with other people and allow yourself to step into the line of their unskilled emotional fire. How could you possibly get to your own work when you are in fix-it mode all the time? You must think seriously about what kind of vehicle your community is for helping you achieve your dreams.

Many people think that the quality of their interactions with friends, bosses, family, and acquaintances is not something they have control over. After all, they choose to act irresponsibly, and you can't help it. In part, that's true. You may not be able to change people, but you certainly can control the amount of time you spend in their presence, or what scenarios you will and will not participate in with them. Having a support network that is a pleasure to be around makes your whole life work better and feel joyful. But that's only half the process. You must also be willing to downgrade the people who are unhealthy for you to a more distant circle, by seeing them less, finding ways to deny them from treating you badly, and otherwise keeping them where they won't bother you as much. Making more room for positive people and less for the negative ones is your mission now. This strategy seems obvious, yet it will take work, changing habits, and using the same laserlike honesty as at the other stops to make your most life-affirming carpool a reality.

Just like an actual office carpool, the one you choose in your life will either help you get to work on time, feeling centered and happy, or make you late, irritable, and throw off your whole day.

Far from being random, each person who enters your life is an invitation—a chance for you to decide with awareness, using the tool of discernment, if each of them will improve the trip of your life or drag it down.

Vacancy/No Vacancy

The central jewel of any healthy relationship, whether it's romantic, familial, friendship, or work-related, is that the vacancy sign is flashing. As at a roadside motel that has rooms available, there should be an underlying feeling of welcomeness—into the heart, the mind, and the life of the other person. You should hear and feel from him or her, "I have room for you, and I want you here." And you should feel like you want that person in your life, too.

Both people in the equation should feel as if they're saying a resounding yes to the relationship the majority of the time, that both people desire to be there and that at the appropriate levels, they want to keep the partnership growing and moving forward. The main thing to look for in your carpool is a sense of evolving, that each rider is involved joyfully and consistently in the process of upgrading his or her respective self, and is in support of the others' being the best they can be as well.

In a healthy relationship, both partners put energy into themselves and, at the same time, find joy in offering something that the other person needs to thrive. For example, it's not balanced to have two partners doing great inner work yet fighting every night. Then you're both getting a No Vacancy sign and you'll feel, rightfully so, that there's not enough room for you at the inn.

So let's flip the scenario. You're actively involved in promoting your own well-being, and that of those around you. You can now not only expect but demand brightly lit vacancy signs from those you allow into your life. I'm not talking diva demanding, nor am I saying that you will get what you need to be content from another person one hundred percent of the time—you won't. You'll be happiest when you allow other people to be human yet, over a period of time, are being positively met more often than not.

I am asking that you set a lovingly firm boundary in your life, that you will not allow people to be in your closest carpool who consistently flash No Vacancy signals at you, people who cannot or will not value you highly or treat you with the welcome that you—or anyone else—deserves.

Vacancy qualities include:

- Trustworthiness
- Consistency
- Being supportive
- Positivity
- Generosity
- Forgiveness that requires personal growth to enable healing
- Remaining loving in both hard times and good ones
- Understanding
- Respectful boundary setting to keep individual needs met
- Compliments for positive actions and attributes
- Being fun-loving and abundant in attitude

No-vacancy qualities include:

- Untrustworthiness
- Inconsistency

- Being unsupportive
- Negativity
- Witholding love
- Being judgmental or critical in ways that do not promote growth
- Becoming distant and angry in hard times
- Rigid insistence on only one perspective of the "truth"
- Selfish boundaries that shut out the other person to maintain individual needs

Guess what? Some or all of these qualities, positive or negative, show up in any relationship—even the best of them. That's because of the following very important road rule: nobody's perfect.

I'm tired of the word *perfect*, anyway. What's perfect? Your idea of it? Mine? No one really knows, but everyone seems to want it. Maybe perfection doesn't exist. Maybe *this* is perfect right now, since it's exactly what you've summoned to help you become who you are. Or maybe perfection means it's the perfect time to use this moment, this experience, to think, feel, and act in the best way you know how, and return to the center of your soul. Regardless, no one can be exactly what you need and want, all of the time.

When choosing your carpool, make sure you don't shut people out just because they're not flashing "vacancy" for you every second of the day, or second-guessing every single need. Could you do that with others? Note that one of the positive qualities in a person is to be able to forgive imperfections and move forward. It's only when there is too much drama, and too little growth, that any relationship can become a roadblock. So, in your carpool, open the door for those whose vacancies outweigh the No Vacancy moments by a broad margin.

Road Rule

Most times, black is not the answer. White is not the answer. Gray is the answer. Find the win-win compromise, and you've found center.

The 80/20 Rule

In college, I went on many a diet, to try to dissolve the freshman 15: no carbs, only carbs, macrobiotic, vegan, the hamburger diet, the Diet Coke diet. I tried, and failed them all. When I found myself starving, eating an entire concession-size bag of peanut M&M's while working out on the step machine in the gym, I knew it was time for a more rational plan.

I went to the university nutritionist, who taught me the all-important 80/20 rule: eighty percent of the time, focus on eating healthfully; twenty percent of the time, go ahead and eat that double-chocolate dessert. Fudge a little, literally.

I suggest that you aim for a carpool in which everyone closest to you is lit with a vacancy sign the majority of the time. Then allow for a minimal amount of negativity in these individuals, without having to throw away the relationship.

In yoga, we say that issues, resistance, and troubled times are as powerful a teacher as the happy ones—and often, more powerful, since you are more compelled toward change in times of discomfort. Welcome these moments of intensity as growth opportunities. Just remember that they should be *moments*—not lasting, or occurring often enough to override your road trip's direction or your general happiness for too long.

take the wheel
Making Your Carpool *Rule*

When it comes to setting up your carpool, know that there are a few nonnegotiables. Some relationships are toxic to you, and you know which ones they are, because you're miserable in them most of the time. They must be removed as entirely as possible. Certain people are wonderful and probably deserve more trust, more attention, and a deeper bond with you. Make that happen. Finally, you can have friends whom you revere but you also remain slightly closed to. It is not a spiritual ideal to let careless people run all over you just because you care about them. You can set boundaries and still love well.

The following sections describe a few techniques to help you field the complexities of your relationships and discern your best carpool for where you are today.

Carpool Meditation

The following meditation is a simple two-step process you can use to clarify who gets to ride in your closest carpool and who gets left behind.

Step 1

1. Get some notecards. On each card, write the name of a person in your life now who you consider to be a major influence on your emotional state, either positive or negative. Do this for every relationship you have: lovers, family, work, friends, acquaintances.

2. Find a comfortable seat. Close your eyes and do two minutes of slow, deep *ujjayi* breathing through your nose.

3. Sit with each notecard. Keep the person in your mind's eye. Without censoring or judging, what feelings arise in you around this relationship? Do you inherently feel it is healthy for you, or not? Why? Write down your first impressions of each person on the back of the card, without editing, as you go. When you've got everything down, move to the next person.

4. When you're finished writing about everyone, do a thymus reset and breathe for two minutes to balance your energy.

Step 2

Put each person's card into one of the following categories, for which I've included some descriptions:

Most intimate. Those you trust above all, with regard to safety, true love, respect, partnership, support, home (lovers, best friends, positive family.)

Very close. Those you love dearly but with whom you may not have as supreme a bond as those in your most intimate group. You still can be vulnerable with them, although not as much time is spent intimately around this group.

Close. Good friends or supporters you can count on, more caring than loving, with whom to begin to set more energetic boundaries.

Professional. People you have work-related relationships with, or those who serve your career goals.

Acquaintance. People you don't know well but still enjoy running into.

Negative but necessary. People who consistently evoke bad feelings in you, yet you must continue to relate to them for some reason.

Toxic. Those past or present relationships, whether love is involved or not, that are disruptive and destructive to your body, your heart, and/or your emotional stability.

When you arrange these categories in circles, originating with you in the center, and moving out from intimacy, and so on, you have your carpool. Come back to this meditation at times, and see if anything's changed.

Now that you know what your carpool looks like, you will want to invite in those closest to you and invite farther out those who you need more distance from.

The Invitation

Gather some markers, glitter glue, and a few sheets of nice paper. For those in your intimate and very close circles, I want you to actually create some invitations into your heart. They are symbolic of those people you will now spend the most attention on, the positive people who make you feel good about being you, most of the time. Make two and give one to the invitee, if you want. Keep your set in a special place to remind you of who loves you for who you are, and who you can concentrate the most fully on instead of moving in unhealthy circles.

The *Out*vitation

Now that you're seeing more clearly who goes in which circle, you may realize you've been expecting things from some people who don't fulfill your desires, or you were treating them as if they were in a different circle. To move someone to a farther-out place, you may have to ask the person to leave or demote them in your heart. Let's deal with the two negative circles: negative but necessary, and toxic.

Negative but Necessary

If a person isn't someone you're intimate with, you might not even have to say anything. You can simply deal with them less, whoever they are. Just change your timing, your presence, and your heart's availability to avoid as much emotional or physical contact with them as possible. Changing jobs or schedules, seeing certain people less frequently, spending more time doing what fulfills you rather than going out of your way for someone, setting a boundary concerning what you'll discuss with this person, expecting less from him or her, or learning to say no to more of another's requests are some ways to shift negative people to a different circle.

A secret to reorienting yourself within negativity is found in ancient Tibetan wisdom, which teaches that no matter how anyone else chooses to act, you still must hold your integrity and act toward him or her with understanding and compassion. You don't have to stick around and take more abuse, but when you react, pause, then re-act from the best of yourself. Often, when you do this, an alchemy occurs. Negative energy cannot coexist for long in the much more powerful light of the soul. You may see relationships transform simply because you literally lightened up the situation. Sometimes people start being more of who you see in them. Sometimes not. Either way, you can choose to walk away with your virtue intact. Write down some creative ways you can do less for these relationships and more for yourself and for those in your closer circles.

When interacting with a person, if you are consistently:

- Unhappy or stressed out much of the time
- Being abused mentally, emotionally, physically, or sexually
- Not feeling respected and cherished
- Losing excitement or drive to be in the relationship
- Feeling that the other person is not invested equally in your partnership
- Inherently misaligned with the person's greater goals and needs

you may want to consider seriously limiting the amount of time you spend with this person or moving on to a relationship that is more balanced and healthy for you. It's not easy to let go of lovers, friends, or acquaintances who are no longer serving a positive purpose in our lives or whose time of teaching has passed. We love people, and love can be hard to walk away from. So can the diseased forms of love, such as codependence, longing, and addiction. It's the greater, more powerful love—the love of self—that you must protect above all else to have soulful partnerships in the future. Your life's trip is too short. And you will thank the universe later for saying good-bye to toxic people now.

Toxic

People don't have to be mean to be toxic—their time with you might just be up, and together you are immersing yourselves in dead energy, even if it's only one of you who feels it's over. Everyone we relate to is our teacher. Each person gives us lessons all the time: lessons we take on in order to learn about ourselves as strong, wise, open-hearted beings capable of great things. Sometimes, though, these relationships are meant to last only a short time. That's a hard concept to swallow in our culture, where such importance is placed on finding a long-term relationship. A thirty-year marriage can be amazing, but it would decrease suffering by the trunkload if we could also see the same inherent value in our shorter-term relationships, and not strive to make everything last forever.

If you know a relationship is over for you, or not healthy, don't be selfish. I say selfish because if you really care about this other person, even as a fellow human being, then you must be the brave, far-seeing one and stand strong through the process of letting go. Your partner deserves the chance to meet the person who will adore him or her, or, if this person's actions were harmful, the opportunity to see that you will not tolerate such treatment, which may lead to his or her healing. Again, let's take a cue from the Buddhists and learn to love what we have that's right for us, *right now,* and be the best people we can, without hanging on and creating suffering if or when the two energies of a relationship become misaligned and need to go their separate ways. Clearing the way for joy to arrive means you have to release what is no longer in alignment within you, or you won't get the next, better relationship. So if you're hanging on, ask yourself if it's worth it—for both of you.

Road Rule

Possibility, like love, seeks a space to fill. How can you make more room right now?

Carpool Nights

Set aside at least two hours, twice a week, to spend quality time with members of your carpool. This should include your partner if you have one and, on another day, members of your close family or friends. Relationships are living entities, a third being created from the actions of two people, and they require an investment of time and attention to thrive. Life is hectic, and it's easy to let responsibilities and stress take you farther away from your carpool. But remember, the people in your support network are one of your first priorities, because they nourish you when you need it most.

Do you know how it feels to be exhausted from work, then meet up with a group of friends, and within a few moments you feel alive again? A proper carpool connects you to spirit, to the very soul of life. Make a point of having a date with your partner, family, or friends twice a week, and you'll be investing in a living stock whose returns are priceless.

What can you do on your carpool nights? Here are some suggestions:

- Have an intimate at-home dinner date and dress way up. Or throw a dinner party for your best friends.

- Go out for bowling or bingo. They're not just for retirees anymore. Plus, you could win money.

- Mani/pedi, anyone?

- Go see the action or horror movie that's good only because a hundred other people are there.

- Try karaoke, especially if you can't sing.

- Go out dancing, especially if you don't dance.

Fourteen Days of NICE:
No Injurious Criticisms Expressed

If you're asking for the best people in your carpool, then you'd better be on your best behavior, too. Acting injurious (harmful, hurtful, or destructive) is something to avoid when steering toward positive relationships. For two weeks, starting right this second, I want you to refrain from letting anything escape your mouth that will cause pain, distance, or shame. Don't blame, or demean other people even if they're not in the room, even if you feel they have it coming. If you have to say something negative, say it nicely. Even if you feel someone else is doing something hurtful to you on purpose, and therefore a negative reaction from you is justified, you can still choose to get your point across with integrity and remain in full abundance.

So for fourteen days, do not speak in any tone of voice or emit comments that are passive, aggressive, or passive-aggressive and are meant to accuse, provoke guilt, or otherwise prove to anybody how much he or she upset or irritated you. This includes gossip, yelling, anger, whining, bitching about anything, speaking harshly, criticizing, or using a "you did this to me" tone of voice. I mean it—no blaming, no quiet demeaning, no separatist techniques, no icy silences, no pouting, no theatrics. You may get angry and feel like being critical or judgmental, but take an adult time-out, then find a way to express what you really need to say from an appreciative, compassionate, and understanding place rather than an agitated one. In this way, you'll teach yourself to redirect those reactive or habitual energies in a more constructive way.

For fourteen days, say whatever you have to with the following intentions behind it: healing, unity, trust, appreciation, curiosity, integrity, respect, compassion, and support. Yes, you can do this even if you need to ask for a change or express that you're hurt or angry. You don't have to say mean things to speak your mind. You may even have to decline to participate in conversations that turn to gossip, or in dramas involving judgment and negative talk. It may be hard to leave the ladies' room snickerfest, but if you don't want it, don't put it out there.

Road Rule

Karma is a boomerang. What you throw out there will come right back at you later.

When going NICE, do one of two things:

1. Find a respectful way to turn a negative dig into a respectful comment.

2. Focus your comment on something that you find positive about the situation.

For example:

> *Not so nice:* "Um, your new boyfriend, 'Moose'? Yeah, the biggest jerk in the world. And what a slob! No wonder he's named after an animal."

> *Nice 1:* "I have to be honest—I'm not feeling a great vibe from Moose. I trust your judgment, and I hope it turns out fine. But if you ever need to talk, I'm here."

> *Nice 2:* "You seem happy, and that makes me happy. Congratulations." (After all, you're not dating Moose, and she is glowing.)

Use the NICE technique with your mate, boss, co-workers, family, and friends, and you will find that the universe showers *you* with more love and integrity. This technique will benefit the people around you, but it's also a powerful way for you to amplify your self-esteem. All of the people I've looked up to refused to speak ill of their fellow beings, period. If they had an opinion, they shared it, but it was never meant to harm. Try it. As soon as your two weeks are up, perhaps you'll want to become NICE-r for a longer period.

Out of all of the things selecting your carpool asks of you, exactly zero are easy. Yet stepping up to the challenge will make space for a surround of love and possibility in your life, and there will be times you have to summon all your strength and let go of past relationships to face these tasks. Only you will know when to hang on and when to open that same hand to wave good bye.

So be brave and turn with all your energy and time toward choosing and loving those people who do the same for you. Even if you have to go solo for a while, until you find the fellow riders who work best for you, it will be a more rewarding trip than settling for anything—or anyone—less.

the treasure cove

Discovering Wealth in All the Right Places

Keeping the Coin

When I was in high school, a friend's family offered me a fabulous opportunity. Their daughter, Kelly, and I were best friends, and because teenage girls as a rule cannot simultaneously enjoy a family vacation and be separated from their entire posse, I was drafted along for the ride. Besides, it was spring break, a beachfront condo in Fort Lauderdale awaited us, and it was by far the most glamorous thing I'd ever been invited to. I was very excited.

My parents, however, refused to let me go. Money was tight that year, and they couldn't afford to have me spend some of it frivolously on tanning oil, dinners at beachfront cafés, glow-in-the-dark T-shirts, and so forth.

I was distraught. I promised to find a job when I returned to pay my parents back for their charity donation, if I could just please go. My father relented, knowing as he did my delusions of grandeur and perhaps wanting to avoid any future dramatics over the long, landlocked Iowa summer.

The first day Kelly's family and I arrived in Ft. Lauderdale, I marveled at the sparkly sea, the tans, and the slight secret smiles on everyone's faces, as if the ocean had been whispering things to them that no one else knew about. I felt the hardest part of myself, the one that had just hunkered down against the brutal midwestern winter, begin to melt in the sun and soak away into the bare feet–worn wood of the boardwalk.

That evening, sporting my first ever sunburn, cooling in the breeze, I stumbled with Kelly across the Tiki Village. This place was total kitsch everywhere I looked, with its Hawaiian-themed straw thatch roofs built right on the beach, overflowing with 3-for-$1 or 5-for-$2.50 plastic leis, bracelets made out of fluorescent dice that spelled one's name, and seashell bracelets, necklaces, even wallets.

In the far corner of this tchotchke heaven stood a tiki-torchlit hut, with a different sign. No quantity discounts here—this one read "Find Pirate Treasure!" I was drawn to it instantly, with its promise of finding a mossy doubloon among a bunch of worthless junk. For the price of thirty lime-green leis, I could try my luck at treasure hunting!

I paid my dollars and wished hard for the treasure to be mine. I reached down deep inside a fountain that held a pirate's chest full of fake coins. I closed my eyes and pictured my fingers finding the real one in all of it, and when I felt something harder than the rest, somehow different, I pulled it up. It was a shiny gold coin, fake like the rest—but on this one, it read in ancient pirate calligraphy: "You found treasure . . . $20!"

The college kid at the counter looked surprised when I brought my bounty up to show him. He shrugged and opened the cash register, but I interrupted the transaction by saying, "That's okay. I don't want the money—I just came up to ask if I could keep the coin."

He looked at me as if I was crazy, but I felt in my heart that this reminder of wishing for something, moving toward it, trusting myself, and then pulling treasure out of a lot of worthless metal, was the real reward. I knew that if I could remember this process and lesson forever, I would not want for money again. And I have remembered. To this very day, my goal is to never exchange the real riches I receive for the quick return. I know the difference, and I know where and how to find more. I've learned that if I reach inside myself, focused and sure, I can draw money out of the universal chest and watch it grow almost magically into a whole pile of treasure that I can share abundantly with myself and my world. Many before me have known the following wisdom from Socrates to be true:

> I do nothing but go about persuading you all, old and young alike, not to take thought for your persons or your properties, but and chiefly to care about the greatest improvement of the soul. I tell you that virtue is not given by money, but that from virtue comes money and every other good of man, public as well as private.

the map
The Treasure Chest Is You

We've talked a lot about relationships by now—those between you and yourself and you and other people. This chapter is about the relationship between you and cash—that often resisted, yet voraciously desired bunch of green paper. You will now begin to forge a healthy relationship with this materialized energy and learn to use it toward things that help rather than harm.

To cease money dysfunction, which is really just another way to say you are not fully opening the treasure chest of your soul to attract positivity on all levels, you must become further acquainted with alignment and abundance. These two concepts, when acted out into your life, will change the way you look at money—and you will be able to include it as a healthy part of your most soulful path.

Alignment

1. To adjust to improve the response over a frequency band, as to align the tuned circuits of a radio receiver for proper tracking throughout its frequency range, or a television receiver for appropriate wide-band responses

2. To adjust (parts of a mechanism, for example) to produce a proper relationship or orientation

Abundance

1. An extremely plentiful or overly sufficient quantity or supply

2. Overflowing fullness: abundance of the heart

3. Affluence; wealth; the enjoyment of abundance

As you can see, at their roots, these two terms describe stepping into the full stream of life—something you say you want to do if you are reading this book. But if you refuse to attract or enjoy money, or see the gift it can be when it is put into the right hands, you are not going along with your own plan. And on all levels, you will face some degree of restriction and lack because your resistance to richness on the outside is really coming from a place within you that is stubbornly stuck in regard to your own wholeness.

Just for fun, read two more definitions:

Health

1. The overall condition of an organism at a given time

2. Soundness, especially of body or mind; freedom from disease or abnormality

3. A condition of optimal well-being: concern about the ecological health of the area

4. Financially secure and functioning well

Wealth

1. Happiness, also prosperity in abundance of possessions or riches

It is interesting that happiness is a state of inner wealth, and the word *wealth* originally meant happiness. We have to go back to the year 1250 for that definition, before too many people with ego-driven desires started giving money a bad name and many of us came to believe it.

Here in the treasure chest, I am not going to tell you where or how to invest your money or give you a savings plan. There are plenty of financial gurus who can help you. I am not going to promise you specific amounts of cash, either. Rather, as one of your spiritual guides, I am going to tell you the energetic laws of how to be financially and, therefore, spiritually abundant, and vice-versa, so you can avoid all the false and worthless advice you may run across on the subject. I will teach you how to understand the true nature of money: how it flows and why sometimes it goes. When you know this information, you'll unlock the mystery of your own cash-flow situation, see why many people don't have the amount they want, and learn how you can use the spiritual principles of energy flow to give yourself the best shot at creating as much financial freedom in your own life as possible. In the meantime, you'll be living in wholeheartedness. And that, my friend, means you're already rich.

After you understand the ways in which you're blocking money from flowing in and learn how to open and redirect the flow according to your wishes, then you can deal with where to stash your cash. But first things first. The treasure chest contains the secrets of how to make money either come to you—or move away. Once you know these secrets, you will never lack for money again or, if you do, you'll know why, and you'll be able to do something about it.

I'd like you to ask yourself a question, and answer very honestly: Does the fact that this spiritual guidebook includes a chapter about money make you uncomfortable? If so, you're not the only one. When I first began envisioning the road trip, I was advised by some colleagues not to include this topic in this book. It made some in the book industry nervous, too; they didn't see a place for "material" things in a "spiritual" book. Some of my friends and clients thought I should leave it out completely, since many people equate money with greed, power imbalances, cruelty, poverty, and nonenlightened views.

I beg to differ. The reality we experience as our lives is in part a material one, and I think we should be able to have an intelligent conversation about money. It is a necessary part of our lives; we depend on it, and we work to get it, yet we're not supposed to know how to align it to our highest goals? To have a harmonious relationship with money will only help you clear the path toward your big yes. We use money to pay rent, eat, perhaps drive and maintain a car. We receive money as an exchange for the services we provide, which in turn helps us to provide comfort, entertainment, and shelter for the world, our loved ones and ourselves. "Material" simply means that money has become an aspect of our intentions that we can see, touch, and feel. These qualities don't make it inherently bad or good—it just *is*.

Money, clearly, is only one of the aspects of what yogis call *artha*, or the great treasure chest. *Artha* describes a state of total inner and outer wealth—not solely material assets, but all kinds of others, such as love, knowledge, happiness, and friendship. It is one of the four *purusarthas*, or goals of life.

It's great to know that when dealing with money, we're really working on a state of total wealth-consciousness that benefits us on all other levels. As the singer Madonna pointed out, we are living in a material world—yet we're also conscious beings who wish to be a positive influence on the planet. Doesn't it make sense to make the world a better place by using both our financial and spiritual powers? Does money have a positive aspect to it, and can we use it in an enlightened way? Can or should we even delight in our money and let it be another source of happiness and joy? I say yes, absolutely yes, to all of the above, and many ancient and contemporary spiritual masters agree. I've included many quotations about money in this stop, so you can see that when you decide to embrace cash, you're in good company.

What is the possible role of money in the lives of people who want to live in harmony and have an abundant cash flow, and yet not contribute to the destructive deci- sions made in the world today around wealth? If you have a deep belief that money is evil, you are bolstering to that very mind-set. When you live as if you love and welcome your money, you will proliferate a positive cash con- sciousness, and your inner and outer worlds will turn to gold.

> *Every time you spend money, you're casting a vote for the kind of world you want.*
>
> —ANNA LAPPÉ, O, THE OPRAH MAGAZINE, *JUNE 2003*

For an especially useful teaching on wealth, let's turn to the Tibetan Buddhist Geshe Michael Roach's book *The Diamond Cutter*. In it, Roach tells how he spent many years in the New York City diamond trade—one of the most cutthroat businesses in the country. At the request of his teacher, he moved from Tibet back to the United States, started in an entry-level job, and worked his way into ownership of a corporation that grew to be worth mil- lions of dollars, all by conducting himself according to the highest Buddhist ideals. He saw firsthand the kind of positive prosperity that can happen when one brings unwaverable personal integrity into even the most challenging world of finance. Roach writes:

There is a belief prevalent in America and other Western countries that being successful, making money, is somehow wrong for people who are trying to lead a spiritual life. In Buddhism, though, it is not the money which is in itself wrong; in fact, a person with greater resources can do much more good in the world than one without. The question rather is how we make the money; whether we understand where it comes from and how to make it continue to come; and whether we have a healthy attitude about the money. As long as we do these things, making money is completely consistent with a spiritual way of life; in fact, it becomes part of a spiritual way of life.

In other words, money is not inherently bad. How you invite it into your life, how you relate to it, and then what you do with it is what counts.

In that same vein, wouldn't people who have good intentions but who also have money embody goodness? I believe so. If you have loving intentions, you can use money as a powerful way to balance out those in the world who are selfish and greedy. If not you, then who? In this way, money becomes a protective energy meant to bring you, your loved ones, and the larger community into a state of abundance and sharing. Money can be a conscious way to help rather than harm.

Road Rule

Money isn't the root of all evil; people with evil intentions *with money* are.

Keep Some, Give Some

Abundance teachings also encourage us to make good money doing what we love—lots of money, if possible—and along with making offerings to help the world, to keep some of it to enjoy in our own lives. The happier and more free you are, the more you'll add that energy to the collective. So fill your treasure chest to overflowing. As you begin to magnetize more material wealth into your life, don't forget to donate some to good causes, but also go on that vacation and finance the life you love.

What Is Your Positive Balance?

The state of your finances is an outer representation of what's going on inside your heart and mind. Whether you do or don't have money can be a source of either freedom or constriction. The key is knowing how much cash flow you require to be able to do the things you want in your life, stabilize yourself and your family, and still have enough to help others. This is a balancing point you will have to find for yourself.

Money can't buy happi-ness ... but neither can poverty.
—LEO ROSTEN

One imbalance around money happens whenever your financial situation causes you or those you love to worry and strain. Your money should be a source of bliss, not stress. A good rule of thumb is: if your money is stressing you out, it's diverting the flow of all other good things to you as well.

Write down on a sheet of paper the amount of money you'd like to make in a year to feel stress-free. Include enough for saving, buying the things you need, paying off your bills, having some fun, and helping others. Post that amount where you can see it, and keep it in your mind. Next you'll learn how to keep it in your heart, too.

Many people make the mistake of thinking that merely accumulating lots of money is what's going to make them happy. Placing your happiness on external material things is never a good idea. Nor does being broke does represent some kind of spiritual ideal. So strike the perfect balance for you—from the inside out. Doing so will add another, deeper level to your financial practice that will bring you the comfort, and the cash, you seek.

Money Inside Out

It seems like money appears from outside of you, but, in reality, it is invited into your life in exact proportion to how much you want it, welcome it, and feel abundant *internally*. To magnetize more money, begin by keeping your perspective turned toward the riches that are within and all around you now, regardless of your current financial situation.

Right now, notice and feel grateful for your kids, your friends, your health, your new haircut, the sunset, football, whatever reminds you that life is pretty darned good, after all. Dwell only on what you appreciate—there is no quicker way to begin welcoming to you prosperity in all forms. Whatever you're thankful for, take it in and feel it—today and for every single day afterward. If you stay in an inner state of fullness, feeling lucky to be alive and dancing in joy about the little things, then you will begin to attract happier materialized energy in the form of money and opportunities to make more of it, too.

Road Rule

Money is an outward manifestation of your inner state; so keep your heart, mind, and spirits in a positive balance, and more money will appear.

Having enough money to enjoy your life and still help others is one aspect of true freedom, so search for, find, and become more flush on the inside—in every possible moment.

Start an Affair with Cash

I do not call it your "relationship to money" for nothing. The laws of love and respect work the same way, no matter whether you're dealing with people—yourself, your lovers, your friends—or your dollars. Treating money as if it were another important person in your life will help you see more clearly where you've blocked money from coming in and staying with you more, and uncover where the imbalances lie. In other words, if you want money, you are going to have to begin to keep your money affair in order, and court it like a potential mate.

To have a money affair, you'll need to add a significant other named Cash to your list of intimate relationships. Cash gets a seat in the innermost circle of your carpool, and if you treat him right, you will have a lifelong supporter who will never let you down. If you want to make money, you have to befriend your money, love your money—and be as good a partner to Cash as you are to your most cherished loved ones. How fully and positively you invest yourself in this affair is exactly how your money will return that investment back to you.

If Cash was an actual person, how have you been treating him? Have you used and abused him at times, loved him one minute, then ignored him or cursed his name and been angry at him for not wanting to be around? Have you made a welcoming space for Cash in your life, or have you been resisting him all along? So many of us say we want money, but given the way we act toward it, if we were dating Cash, he might have dumped us, and for good reason. Ask yourself: Have I been treating my money as a friend or as an enemy?

The Wealth Equation

We all know that being poor tends to promote misery. Yet there are also people in the world who have made fortunes and are equally as miserable. And there are those who want more money but can't seem to get it, and those who have money but have no idea how to wisely use it toward their goals. This confusion results because all of these people are lacking in one part or more of the following wealth equation:

Inner Abundance + Aligned Intentions + Positive Relationship with Cash + Aligned Actions = Money

Let's take the rich man who is still unhappy. He may have the relationship part down. He understands how money likes to be treated, and he acts accordingly. His intentions are aligned with making money, and his actions promote that goal. Money flows in. But his treasure chest is only half-open. The primary means of happiness, being in his life from a place of inner abundance, is lacking, and so anything this man does will not bring him lasting joy. Perhaps he's not passionate about the job he chose to make his money, and, over time, it costs him his health. Maybe he feels empty inside, so he tries to buy happiness through things and collects people who love only his money—and we know how that story ends.

Whatever your financial state—rich or poor or somewhere in between—you must align with all parts of the wealth equation, or you may begin to make more cash, but you will rarely be able to truly enjoy it. Without the joy of living directing your choices, the outer actions and inner experience of money will be dry, lonely, and devoid of the fruit of actions that are born from a place of true love.

Try to live the full wealth equation as often as you can. Money can't buy you happiness, but happiness attracts money. So find ways to become happier first, and you'll dissolve some of your strongest financial blocks. This may sound like a no-brainer, but I can assure you, it's hard as hell to follow. I am asking you here to resist the temptation to wait until you have money to feel great about your life and to release the idea that more money will pay off your state of inner debt. Instead, begin to develop a strong state of inner okayness and worth inside of yourself, even if you've still got bills to pay. When you do this, you will not only open the door for a better financial situation, you will start enjoying all these precious moments you have that you will never live in exactly this way again.

Money as Energy

First, since you're learning to see cash in a more positive light, you must treat yourself to a new, more conscious use of money. Money is simply energy manifested into a physical form you can hold, fold, and put in your wallet. The underlying stuff that makes a dollar bill is the same energy that makes up your body, and your intentions. You don't want to just exist financially—you want to thrive, just like you do with all forms of your soul fuel. Remember the law of thermodynamics? How you begin to direct the flow of your energy/money through spending and/or saving it will immediately affect you on the very deepest level.

How do you personally use this monetary manifestation of energy? Do you keep enough to nourish and sustain yourself and your loved ones—or do you overspend, overcharge, and ignore debts until you're beyond empty and into the negative? Anytime you are in a money deficit, you are also in a life-energy drain. Anytime you lower your inner energy, your money will be affected. Depleting actions will not lead to inner or outer wealth but instead to a comprehensive state of poverty that can show up in other ways in your life as disease, relationship problems, depression, and the like.

Check that you're really honoring and making the choices to use your money as the expression of your soul that it really is. First, get a beautiful wallet and place your money consciously in it. Put a picture of people you love right next to the bills so you begin to relate the two and remember that how you treat your cash should mirror the quality of your other relationships, since what you do with it affects everyone you care about.

The fastest way for you to begin to invite the flow of cash into your life is to do the things you love. I think most people, including you, if given the choice between making money at a job that is somewhere on the spectrum between "I don't care about this" and "I hate it" or doing something they're interested and passionate about, would choose the latter. When you realize you can have money without being negatively attached to it or allowing it to derail you onto some evil track, then perhaps you're ready to read this next thought, one that may be rather shocking: you should be paid well for doing what you love!

You probably read that and thought, "Duh! Of course, I should!" But then is your next thought somewhere along the lines of, "But you can't make money doing _____!" or "I would never make enough to support my family doing _____!" Or, "I don't want to accept money for my art, because then I'll have to compromise," and so on?

If this is the case, you're one of many. How do you think the term starving artist entered our vocabulary? It's an expression most people know, and it was created and sustained by the erroneous belief that people who do what they love cannot make a living at it, especially through their work in the creative arts.

This mind-set applies whether you love to paint on canvas or crunch numbers for fun. Everyone is a creator; everyone has at least one major talent he or she was put on this earth to express, and so few of us make it anything more than a once-in-a-great-while hobby. So many people talk themselves out of their own destinies, or they let someone else tell them that their goal is impossible to achieve.

When I was deciding to leave a lucrative career as a journalist and put all my energy and intention into my career as a yoga teacher and author—of the healing arts, no less—the negative voices began to get louder from every direction, both inside my head and from others—even from people who had never met me before. I heard: "But there's so much competition in that field!" "There's no money in yoga, not to mention books!" "No one reads any more! Good luck." "How can you afford to live in New York City and do that?" And on and on.

Luckily, I also have a fabulous community of family, friends, and clients who gave me a deafening roar of support. But the negative beliefs were strong, too, and I could easily have chosen to let them feed into my fears and keep me from my life's work, forever. Instead, I became quiet, sat with my doubts and, through getting to know them better, realized that just underneath them was a voice saying, "Yes, but what if you never try? Wouldn't you regret it more than anything else?"

I decided to have courage and follow my heart. I began to align my thoughts and deeds more closely with what I dreamed about. To fulfill my greater purpose, I focused on doing what I felt compelled to. I built an income-generating job of directing a yoga studio, while teaching yoga classes and training teachers in my yoga style. I also carved out at least two hours a day to begin writing. I wrote because I felt there was something I needed to say, even before I knew if anyone else would want to read it. And that commitment turned into a book deal with a major publisher and became the reality you are now holding in your hands.

You can turn your passion into a career, too.

What is it you love to do? Put it all down on paper, even the things that may seem ridiculous. I *love*: yoga, writing, relationships, healing arts, philosophy, science, chocolate, metaphysics, finding connections, travel, transforming lives, love. So I decided to do something that encompassed all of these things.

Do you think your passion is too absurd? I have a friend who loves to put beads on a string in a certain order, depending on her mood. She began making glorious bracelets, not knowing what would come next. A few people saw them and she sent out some pictures to a few magazines, and now she sells them for big bucks. She also travels cross-country, teaching others how to make jewelry.

Another friend of mine loved to tell people how to decorate and rearrange their furniture so they can have better energy flow in their lives. Through studying with pros, and beginning with the homes and offices of friends, she became one of the country's leading interior designers. Then there's a woman I know who loves making hats—one at a time, to fit the specific person she meets. A huge national magazine found her, without her even reaching out. From one day to the next, she went from a scared, slightly depressed but hopeful hat maker to a superstar stylist.

All of these people started with a seed passion that they grew into a lifelong, sustainable career. Here's a big secret of wealth, and of your life, too: when you do what you love, even a little at a time, the right path opens for you, and you will find the impossible becoming possible every step of the way.

For this transition to happen, you don't even have to trust in it. You don't have to leave your current job or make any huge decisions. You do, however, have to get started doing

Road Rule

With every small and big action you take toward your dreams, another coin drops into your treasure chest. Soon it will be overflowing!

what you really want to be doing with your life, even on a micro level. If you take a minor action, it will lead to the next, bigger opportunity. Energy, like money, needs your direction in order to know where to flow. The doorway may start by opening just a crack, but it will eventually and, with your commitment, swing wide.

I now disagree with, and in fact, I laugh at, those negative voices. I know from experience, mine and many others, that the universe wants you to share your gift with the world—and the world needs it. It's not enough to be in a good job that makes you good money, if you're not feeling fulfilled on the soul level. We've lost a lot of our idea of what true wealth is, and many people chase or cling to the jobs that pay well—seeking relief on the outside rather than finding ways to be at peace on the inside first. As a spiritual creator, you have a responsibility toward the world to benefit it as much as you can while you're here, so you must first find more ways to benefit yourself.

take the wheel
Your Soul's Checkbook

The spiritual key to developing freedom around money is to make sure that you maintain a positive inner balance instead of a negative one. You must think, feel, and take actions in radical alignment with what you want your preferred outer reality to become.

Here are some popular ways to block the flow of money into your world by acting in contradiction to your intentions. See if you can spot the common thread among them:

- Talking about how broke you are
- Stressing out and worrying about your bills
- Spending more money than you know you have
- Not facing up to creditors or past due bills
- Being embarrassed to receive money, especially for doing what you love

- Believing that money is evil, or that you don't deserve wealth

- Thinking that in order to make good money, you have to work long and hard and give up things you love, such as quality time with your family or sleep

Do you see the pattern? All of these money roadblocks are born from an inner state of negativity I call "lack." Each one of these thinking, feeling, or doing states comes from a root of fear—fear of not having enough, not being capable of doing enough, not being worthy enough. This fear is a nearly universal ailment, and it can incapacitate those who do not prepare for it.

To navigate around a lack mentality, you must change what you think and what you do. Specifically, you must swap any limiting, negative beliefs for those that literally enrich your sense of inner self-worth and, therefore, promote self-wealth. To change these old patterns, you must expose them at their roots and pull them up into the light of your awareness. Only when you know what's holding you back can you hope to move ahead.

You can also use the following exercise to locate and clear any aspect of your heart that feels blocked. Just substitute *relationships* or *myself* for the word *money!*

Step 1: What's Your Story?

What are your beliefs around wealth—what thoughts and emotions does the concept of money bring up, especially negatively? How much wealth do you really think you deserve? What do you think it takes to make money? Do you really trust that you can make a living pursuing what you love? Write down anything and everything that comes up for you around this topic—memories, fears, blocks, everything. All of it is crucial—it is your current story about money, and, therefore, reflects what you are calling into your life. Begin with "My money story is:"

Here's an example. I hold a lot of shame and guilt around money because in my family I never received it without feeling that I was taking something away from my hard-working parents. I learned that to buy frivolous items or go out to dinner was selfish, and so I still don't feel good about doing those things for myself.

Step 2: Change Your Story from Lack to Light

Take the story you just wrote and revise it to become your new, improved outlook. What do you hope for regarding money— enough to help yourself out of debt, with some (or a lot) left over to help your family and friends? Tell yourself how worthy you are of having this kind of abundance. How can you switch your money outlook to a more expansive, positive one?

It's very important that you take a moment to close your eyes and send light in the form of forgiveness to those you feel wronged you around money in the past and also to the places in you that have been operating from a place of lack.

Here's my revised story: I believe that money is abundant, and the more I have, the more I can share. Going out for entertainment makes me feel happy to be alive, and I deserve to be happy. I release any past mistakes made by myself and others. Everyone was doing the best we knew how. Now that I know differently, I will honor my past, present, and future by acting differently. I free myself from all guilt around making or spending money responsibly and, once in a while, treating myself and my friends to some fun. My new mantra is: "I am a money magnet."

Step 3: Live Your Story

To manifest the things you've just written down, you must stick closely to your new story in real life. If you have your revised tale down on paper yet you're still living by your old one, it will continue to guide your experiences. If you begin to make choices and think more along the lines of your new story, those principles will start to show up in your life, as your life. In yoga, the world you see and everything in it is called *maya*, or the world of illusion. Because life isn't static and what you see isn't all there is, illusion plays a role in how you see yourself in the world. Life isn't carved in stone—it's actually more like clay, malleable, and you mold it into various shapes every day with your intentions and movements.

Over time, if you change your money story or any limiting fable you've created, you will begin to reshape your world to have more treasure in whatever ways you, as the sculptor, has chosen. So be vigilant with what you impress upon your world. Illusion or not, you still have to live in it. I want you to enjoy it for as long as you are alive.

What would you need to think, do, or feel differently to make the new story the true tale of your life? Write down all the possibilities and begin to incorporate those changes into your daily routine as soon as possible. Note that I said "daily." To change lifelong patterns and beliefs, you must commit to becoming your rewrite. Repetition makes reality, just as pressing one palm into your clay one time won't make it into a ball, but rolling it between your palms for a few minutes will.

If you dedicate daily to living your shift, you will see bigger changes happen much more quickly. Here's an example. To become more comfortable with spending money on frivolous things, I would first stop calling them frivolous, which feels negative, and instead start calling them fun. Then I'd set aside one night a week as a fun night where I gladly spend some of my money on things I enjoy.

Remember to balance the reality of your current situation with the knowledge that it will take some amount of time for you to accumulate more wealth. I wouldn't suggest buying a Bentley with your life savings right now, just because you're starting to be richer inside. But once you begin to bring in more cash, you can responsibly manage it and maintain your wealthy outlook while you do the right things to keep your money growing. If you want to know more about how to increase and invest your dough, look to my favorite expert, Suze Orman (www.SuzeOrman.com). She's one of our most inspirational leaders in money management today. She'll steer you in the right direction.

How to Discover Treasure

Here are some simple actions you can take to turn your relationship with cash into a healthy one:

Revitalize Your Affair

- Make a personal treasure chest. I have a Buddha statue on my writing desk, and he's holding a candle—and a dollar. It's a statement that I want to keep light around my finances and also use it to promote a higher spirituality in the world. What do you need to keep in mind?

- Keep your spare change in a beautiful jar. Liberate it from dark places like coat pockets and couch cushions. Keep refreshing the jar with change, and cash it in when the jar gets too heavy.

- Make Cash feel not only welcome in your life, but also cherished.

- On that note, here are some ways to make him feel loved, so he will stick around.

Cash Relationship Rules

- Don't chase after Cash; he doesn't like that. Instead, show him he's wanted. Then step back. Give him room to move by knowing what you want to spend him on. Make a list and post it by your treasure chest.

- Don't make Cash feel used or cheap. Plug your leaks where you spend money on things you don't love or don't need. Common areas of leakage include coffee, snacks, alcoholic beverages, impulse buys, anything you bought just because it came in bulk. Do you really need twenty-five pounds of caramel corn?

- Communication with Cash is key. Talk to him; tell him how happy you are to have him around. Thank him for what he buys for you, and let him know you'd love to see more of him. You can do this in your head if you're not in the mood to let your co-workers see you talking to your open wallet. Show your gratitude toward the money that's with you, and Cash will reward you greatly by dropping in more often.

In other words, treat your money the way you'd want to be treated in any relationship with someone you want to stick around. What you're really saying is, "I am honoring money because I am now worthy of having it." That's major.

Bye-Buys

Anytime you spend your supposedly precious money on something you don't need or aren't in love with, you've sent a message to Cash that he's not that important either and you don't care if he goes away. Using your money toward stuff you don't feel anything about or that is unnecessary also causes an energy leak to spring inside of you. It drains you, because your actions are saying, "I am not worthy of using life energy toward powerful things, but I will give it away to things that mean little or nothing to me." I call these purchases the bye-buys, because you're essentially waving away cash every time you spend like this.

Over time, these little things will add up. With a consistent enough habit of bye-buying, you will begin to experience a life-energy drain on the inside and a sluggish money flow on the outside.

Retaining energy is the step just before growth. Before your money can build in strength, you have to show it that you won't spend it on any old thing that comes your way and, most important, that you won't blatantly waste it.

Common Leaks

Here are just a few ways to say bye-buy and deplete your monetary energy. Can you list others that are happening in your life?

- Interest, from unpaid bills, credit cards, and so forth. To me, the word *interest* means, "I just gave you more money for no reason." Letting interest build up each month is like taking a hundred-dollar bill for a drive and then throwing it out the window. For some of you, it's a lot more money. Avoid interest as much as you can by consolidating, paying off bills, and watching what you buy with your credit cards.

- Impulse buys. Most malls and stores are purposefully set up to psychologically influence you to buy things you don't need and might not even want once you get home. Beware, and plan accordingly. Bring a list and get only what's on it.

- Snacks and beverages. Keep a large water bottle or thermos around and refill it with homemade teas, coffee, water with lemon and carry nuts, fruit, or granola bars—anything to keep you away from the vending machine or coffee shop every day.

- Overdoing nights out. Notice how I said "nights." One's okay. But repeatedly going out, buying more drinks than you should, eating because you're tipsy, then buying rounds of $12 drinks for your one-night-only bar friends drives you away from wealth. You'll be shaking your (poor, aching) head—and wallet—in the morning.

There are many more bye-buys, and you'll know (and feel) them when you see them.

Know Your Bye-Buy Equation

For one month, whenever you make a bye-buy, write it down on a list. At the end of the month, add them up. My daily bye-buy equation looked like this:

Chai latte ($2.75) + Water at yoga ($2) + Snacks ($5)
= $9.75 per day

There's more, but just these three seemingly harmless purchases equaled $292.50 per month, or $3,510 per year!

What could I have done with an extra $3,500? Probably a lot. I changed my habits and made a weekly batch of chai and brought some to work in a thermos each morning. I bought a filtered water pitcher and take a bottle with me to yoga. I stopped eating snacks that I didn't need and kept fruit with me in case I got hungry (banana: 25 cents). And with my extra money, I can do something I really want, such as invest it and watch it grow.

Now, I'm not saying you can't buy anything extra. I'm definitely not telling you to think or act cheap. I'm simply saying don't waste money on things you don't really need. Spend smarter. Don't make Cash feel like you don't care where he goes—would you like to be treated like that? You should not skimp on what you enjoy, but balance it and make sure that the things your good money goes toward are really worth it. The money you save in bye-bye areas can grow and be applied toward your dreams.

Make an Offer the Universe Can't Refuse

In my opinion, money's full value is lost if you don't give some to assist your larger community. Even if you offer just a little bit, it creates a void, and more cash will rush to fill a space made from the heart. However, you want to make sure what you're giving it away to holds positive meaning for you. This will begin the cycle of your of having more than enough money, both to keep and to give. Energy will always fill a void, so make a powerful "giving void" by supporting a cause, helping a friend in need, or even donating some of your material things to charity.

Once when I was pretty broke, I decided to sponsor a child from the Dominican Republic through Children International (www.childreninternational.org). It only cost $22 per month, and I wanted to help someone while also showing the universe I was ready to use my money for good. I echoed this in every other way I could think of, though the bills were looming large. Within a week, money started to flow back in from some surprising sources, invitations, and opportunities, and it's never stopped growing since.

Feng Shui Your Cash

I want to take another page from the ancient masters of directing energy and turn to feng shui for one of the most effective ways I've found to invite big bucks through the door: creating a prosperity shrine. I use one at home, and it works. The day I put mine together, I got a check for $1,180 in the mail. A shrine is a spot in your house where you place things intentionally to show their importance to the universe. Do you know the good, welcomed feeling you get when your new boyfriend or girlfriend clears you a space in the closet? Making a property shrine is the same thing, only you're asking abundance to move in.

One feng shui principle states that those things you see every day have the most impact on you. So, ideally, your shrine should be someplace where it catches your eye on a regular basis, perhaps an area you can see before you go to sleep or when you wake up. Or perhaps you will put it near your work space. It should be a daily reminder of your best financial intentions.

According to feng shui, the wealth area or money corner is the far left area of a room, as you come in the main door. Just keep it away from drains, toilets, garbage, dirt, or big piles of bills—all negative influences on cash flow.

The traditional symbols of wealth, such as green, gold, and purple items; coins, and, of course, actual cash, can all go here. But if something symbolizes prosperity more strongly to you, like that villa in France you'd like to afford, an organization you'd like to support, or a large check to yourself, then put that in your shrine, too.

Other Secrets

Since you are working both outside in and inside out simultaneously, you want to make sure that you are thinking thoughts of wealth as you put this stop into action. You should remain committed to the highest good for all people and try to never get greedy or need for others to have less than so that you can have more. There is plenty to go around for us all. So as you focus, let the backdrop for your manifestations of your increased wealth be a catalyst for all others around you to succeed, so that humanity may also benefit from your financial success.

As you create new habits and reap the rewards of your improved relationship with Cash, always remember to check in with yourself once in a while. Are you on or off track with your wealth equation? If you are off, what can you do differently? What is your story about who you are and beliefs about wealth in all areas of your life? Does it need some editing? With even a little attention to your new wealth-consciousness, you will see major transformations occur. You might just get to enjoy that French villa after all!

the magic gardens

How Mastering Health and Healing Can Revolutionize Your Life

my Trip
From Near-Death to Full Speed Ahead

My first road trip would have been a school field trip when I was thirteen. Instead, I found myself lying in a hospital examination room, supposedly dying. I'd been feeling exhausted and was bruising a lot, and when the blood tests came back I was diagnosed with a platelet count so low the doctors assumed I must have advanced leukemia.

For a just-turned teen, this news meant that for the following week, I wandered around my junior high school in a daze, questioning my mortality for the first time, a curious and strange sensation like a new limb that had grown in my sleep. My mother was shocked and tried her best not to scare me further, while asking the doctors for a retest.

Several days passed, and I became very ill, having suffered a seizurelike episode in science class, from which I was pushed through the hallways to the nurse's office, still sitting in my orange plastic chair. Once home, I became so exhausted and dizzy that even breathing was difficult, and laughing or singing was impossible. Along with swollen lymph glands, a sore throat, and a low-grade fever, my joints, muscles, neck, and head ached constantly. I lived on the couch. I crawled to the bathroom. I didn't understand what was happening to me.

After two weeks with these symptoms occurring unabated, we got a call from the hospital. They apologized profusely for a technician's error. I did not have leukemia nor was I dying, though I sure felt like it. But something was terribly wrong. If not cancer, then what was happening to me?

The diagnosis was Epstein-Barr virus, later to become known as the catch-all chronic fatigue immune dysfunction syndrome (CFIDS). Today, twenty-two years later, although progress is being made, there still remains a great deal of mystery surrounding the cause and treatment of this elusive illness. Yet I know from experience the complete debilitation and life-altering consequences of this very real disease.

At first, I thought if I rested, it would go away. Fatigue sounds so simple, so easy to fix. Sleep! How I was mistaken. I found myself in the same boat with millions of other Americans with this virus: the more I rested, the more tired I became. I felt like an unwell ninety year old instead of the energetic girl I could barely remember being.

The color went out of life, and for two years I was in and out of school. I missed much of it, and even when I was there physically, I was not able to concentrate or absorb what my teachers were saying. I slipped from having been an A student to barely passing in a matter of months. I still don't know the basics of algebra or geometry that were taught in those years. During the coming summer, I could not read, talk, or stand for more than a few minutes, and I slept on the couch whenever I was too weak to climb to my top bunk, which was almost every night.

Outside my windows, I heard my former friends laughing, playing, and getting older while I became more alone, more confused, and more frightened of the dark—I knew that unknown place all too well, and I felt more like a ghost when the lights went out. I felt as if I were dying; yet I wouldn't die. Often, I feared my life would be as wasted away as my body, and my spirit longed to be free. I contemplated that freedom and weighed using a razor to end my pain against the pain I would cause those I loved if I did. Reluctantly, I decided to stay and fight.

I realized my illness was not going away unless I did something radically different. It took me until I was a senior in high school before I would discover what that was.

One night, as I was watching the stars from my family's little apartment balcony, trying to find Orion, I had an epiphany. CFIDS was the name of my illness, the way each star had a name. But both CFIDS and stars are made of smaller particles, which join together to form a whole (I must have been in class that day!). What were the particles of my illness? If I could figure out how it was put together, just maybe I could dismantle and reassemble it to make CFIDS into something else, or at least a smaller star in the cosmos of my life. At the time, it was the sun.

But what was at the root of it? What were the elements that caused it to find a home in my body? If I looked beyond the physical manifestation of disease, I could pinpoint a few places where I had come into disharmony with my true nature. My parents divorced when I was eight, and I clammed up—never crying, just building storm clouds of anger inside. Then we moved to another city and I had no friends, which made me more depressed. I stopped eating for a while, preferring my control over food to the lack of control I felt all around me.

So began my frequency disruption, which moved me from a happy space into a dark, negative one. I'd begun an energy drain, which turned severe through high school as I turned to emotionally and sometimes physically abusive partners to match my low self-esteem. I ate horribly—when I ate at all. I overexercised and underloved myself. I hated my parents, who, though imperfect themselves, really loved me. Basically, my life was a mess—a big mess, all perpetuating more lack and disease.

What manifested as a chronic, or ongoing, state of fatigue, I believe, was an end result of all those years of constricting my life flow and vibrating at a dismally low level. I wanted to reopen the gates and raise my vibration any way I could and planned to spend as long as it took finding out if this strategy worked. It had already taken me years to get to this place, but if I could be happier on the inside, maybe over time my outside would begin to match it. I truly had nothing to lose.

To the couch I brought spiritual and self-help books, beginning the studies that would help me see beyond my problems to the source of them. I formed overseas friendships with pen pals, ate better, drank water, tried to do some light daily exercise, walking around the apartment once. I learned yoga breathing and did nightly meditations on healing. I tried anything I could; I even talked to myself in a nicer way when I was too tired to do anything else.

Over time, during my college years, feeling better and more empowered, I swapped my abusive relationships and dead-end jobs for more respectful and rewarding ones. Sometimes I regressed, or felt as if I wasn't making progress, but I remembered that the journey would be long and would appear more like a stretched-out Slinky shape than a straight line. I stubbornly made this regimen a daily routine, and, after a while, I started feeling stronger. I could open a jar of peanut butter by myself again. I could laugh without losing my breath.

My little yoga practice was starting to expand, and I looked more forward to getting up each day. As I made my inner life better, my outer life began to reform to match it. I was hired for a great job at a flower shop. I met a nice guy. When I was tired, I would rest and then continue my healing lifestyle from there. When did a healing lifestyle become my reality? When I decided it would be, sick or not.

Even while ill, I chose to stop thinking about being a sick person and instead developed a mind-set of healing. All day long I assumed I was getting better; when I ran into a limitation, I noticed it, accepted it, rested, and continued my healthy mind-set. At night when I was tired, I'd imagine I'd just done a full day's work—and play—that I loved, and I would go inside, to my mind's quietest place, to thank the universe for the chance to heal. At times, I felt was fooling myself, but I also felt there was only one other option: to believe I was a sick person. This idea I could no longer afford to empower, no matter what the eventual outcome.

Fast-forward ten years: I moved to New York City in 2001 and became a yoga teacher, a writer, and a spiritual adviser to hundreds of people per week in person, and thousands per day online. It may have taken two decades, but today, as a result of years of honing my understanding and practice of health, I am balanced enough to have my own vigorous style of yoga, Core Strength Vinyasa Yoga, aimed at maintaining one's connection to center even while expressing out into the world. I now practice it at least three times a week. I do handstands. I travel the world. I have physically transformed into not only an exceptionally strong and healthy person but have also become a leader in my fields of yoga, mind-body healing, and spiritual guidance, using my gifts and experiences to transform the lives of others.

I live—and thrive—in one of the most intense cities in the world. I mention this not to toot my own horn but in hopes of encouraging you to become more healthy in body, mind, and spirit. If I could do it, so can other people.

I still have the remnants of CFIDS with me, reminding me to slow down, rest, and balance. Some days I need to sleep when my body asks. I don't fight it—I just take a long nap. I've oriented my responsibilities so there's ample room for relaxing.

Because, I believe, of my dedicated healing practice, I am now one of the CFIDS success stories. This disease can last for years, even a lifetime. I strongly suspect, however, that in many cases,

CFIDS can be beaten—from within. I am not promising that you will be cured of anything that ails you, but I'll tell you this: *any* diseased or misaligned body, mind, or heart can be re-attuned for the best possible results, using the principles I will set forth in this stop.

the map
Opening Your Treasure Chest Wide

In the following sections I've provided you the keys to unlock your own vehicle of healing, energizing, and all-around transforming. They were cut from the direct experience of the struggles and victories of my biggest road trip ever—the one I rode over years of time, the one I took inside of me, to find my soul and bring it back from the brink, and with it, myself.

The road I love so much might never have been available to me had I not changed my mind, heart, and, eventually, my body into that of a healthy person. I did it by following a simple energetic equation and developing a discipline of healing.

Whether you have a disease, feel imbalanced, or want to make any aspect of your lifestyle healthier, you will benefit from this stop. You'll learn how it's possible to change your health, and I tell you this from ultimate experience—you *can* heal yourself to a great extent; be a healthier, balanced person; and continue to enjoy your vitality for the rest of your days.

What Is Disease?

The word *disease* originally meant "lack of ease and trouble." If you break it into two parts: *dis* and *ease*, you can see that the root of what we now think of as this illness or that condition really stems from a lack of ease—of balance and harmony predominating—in the life-energy flow. This can happen at the level of your mental, emotional, or physical state. The soul can never truly be touched by any imbalance, but if you heap enough discomfort on top of it, you may get sick and have a tougher time revealing the peace within.

If you are cutting off the flow of positivity, like running out of oil in a car, you risk breaking down on some level. I would like to see you avoid a breakdown or, if you're already in one, to fix it to the best of your ability, and move on.

I count a few things as disease. Anytime you're feeling unhappy, exhausted, anxious, obsessed, upset, out of control, too controlling, depressed, passionless, sick, powerless, or hopeless, or are hating your life, you are getting an emotional clue that you are out of balance and are attracting more disease and less health. Stay in these states for too long, and the disharmony may begin to result in physical or mental manifestations.

Often, diseases are seen as outside invaders, something we cannot prevent or change. Sometimes that may be the case. But often, I think that we unconsciously invite disease as the product we create through our inner states and outer choices along the way. I think that it is much harder for diseases to root and stick in a body that is in alignment on all levels. This central yogic concept underlies the basis for our practice of physical postures, meditation, breathing, and positive intentions.

I am not omnipotent; I don't know all the answers. It's tricky for me to tell you that you can heal yourself on many levels, when there are people who were born blind or paralyzed. Children get cancer, and I don't think they have had enough time to live in misalignment to develop their disease.

I do have a deep sense of the universal ways, however, and through experience, I've learned to trust it. I suspect that some people choose in this lifetime to manifest illness or mental or physical challenges from a place that is wiser than we know. Perhaps they needed to experience it or give a certain experience to those that come into contact with them. Maybe it's just the roll of the dice. We can't know for sure. All we can do is try our best from where each of us is to cultivate that peaceful, easy feeling.

Regardless of whether you are going to heal physically or not, you can develop a more steady inner equilibrium. Then the best possible outcome is assured. When you commune with your soul and deal at the level of pure vital energy, you can absolutely take a major role in the creative process, and you may even be able to diminish or dissipate the disease. You can take action to help tip the balance toward the optimal conditions for healing and health. Start by realigning with the opposite of disease: ease.

Yogi Body, Yogi Mind

The Sanskrit term for "ease" is *sukha*. Its deeper meaning, however, is "a good state or space." The way I see it, you do one of two things in each moment—move toward health or away from it, depending on whether you are in a good heart and mind space or not. You are going to use your energy toward something in every moment, so why not make that something life enhancing instead of life destroying?

Many yogis know that disciplining oneself to keep the body fit and flexible, the mind at center, and the heart in freedom helps the student maintain a positive energy balance. If a student veers into imbalanced energies, which really means letting negative vibrations become predominant, for too long, a state of disease can manifest in the body. To counter this fate, you must master balance.

In yoga, we know that a body, mind, or heart that works too hard can be just as unhealthy and prone to disease as one that doesn't work hard enough, so the student is encouraged to become skilled at this balancing dance to find the workable-enough center between the two.

Practice may not "make perfect," as the saying goes, but it can certainly make a whole lot of shifts happen. No matter what is causing you to feel ill, upset, or fatigued now, through a dedicated practice of healing intent and harmonious actions, you can have the best shot at overcoming it.

The Roman poet Ovid said, "*Gutta cavat lapidem,*" which means "Dripping water hollows out a stone." He understood that repetitive action creates a form and can also change a form into something other than what it was before. To "practice" something or to have a "discipline" is really just to take enough repetitive action to make a difference in some direction. If you're interested in getting or remaining as healthy as possible, you need to know the direction you want to go in and then *do* something about it— every day.

The roots of good health are identical to those of attracting wealth. They seem different only because they manifest differently: one into a sound mind and body, the other into financial abundance.

The key to seeing the parallel is to think about life energy as an investment. When you invest in something, you give it money in the hopes that it will provide more money in return. You would probably not invest in a stock, for example, that you know will fail and leave you broke. That seems obvious. But, in fact, many people do exactly that every day: they spend their life energy on things that give them no return or actually drain out more energy than was originally put in. Directing your attention, actions, or emotions toward any person, place, or thing that puts you in an energy deficit is likely to provide a negative return in the form of energetic bankruptcy, an emotional, mental, and physical breakdown and, eventually, the manifestion of an imbalance, illness, or even disease.

To cut your losses, you must withdraw your energy from the losing investments, and reinvest in those things that provide you with a positive return (anything that puts you in a good mood is a good start). When we spend our life energy wisely, we begin to feel more energetic, passionate, and excited about living. This happens because we are becoming wealthy on the inside— having an abundance of life force that keeps flowing in, so we can offer some of it and still retain some in our personal life-saving account to remain in balance.

Look at and write a page about your own life-saving account—your general balance of energy in and out. Have you been chronically spending past zero, relying on energy loans from

other people to bail you out, becoming overdrawn with prom-
ises and responsibilities, or even going completely bankrupt with
exhaustion? I would say that at the pinnacle of my CFIDS, I was
filing energy Chapter 11. I was about as far down as a human
being could go. Only when I started to take actions to keep me
in a positive energetic balance each day would I end a day in the
black, rather than in the red, and finally begin to turn my illness
around.

The main cause of life-energy deficits that can manifest as
disease is that the investor—in this case, you—has made a geo-
metric error. You've been drawing lines with your energy instead
of circles.

Black Elk, a renowned Native American medicine man of the
Sioux tribe, once said:

> You have noticed that everything an Indian does is in a
> circle, and that is because the Power of the World always
> works in circles. . . . Even the seasons form a great circle in
> their changing, and always come back again to where they
> were. The life of a man is a circle from childhood to child-
> hood, and so it is in everything where power moves.

Black Elk was talking about a very profound concept here:
the way energy travels. When we envision the flow of energy, it
sounds like a river—going one way, in a straight line. That's misleading. If your energy is going one way only—only inward or
only outward, an imbalance will result. If you have too much
energy coming in, and no proper outlet, you can develop nervous disorders, such as anxiety or obsessive worry. If you have too
much energy going out and you're not keeping enough in reserve,
you risk fatigue, depression, and a poorly functioning immune
system.

A secret to life is that optimal life energy actually flows in a
circle: both in and out of you at the same time, with the spiritual
source being the universe and its biggest healer: love. Like your
physical circle of breathing, you continually draw in life energy,

and yourself, to the source and you send it back out as your personal expression. This profound concept is understood not only by the wealthy but also by the healthy, who honor its wisdom by making it their conscious discipline.

The key to healing is to send out your energy (or invest it) in ways that draw positive energy back into your being (a healthy return).

Arguing with someone uses many, many dollars' worth of your energy but gives you about fifty cents in return. Have you felt emotionally broke after a big fight? Then you've experienced the truth of this equation. Having a loving, compassionate, and fruitful conversation with that same person about the same issue uses energy, yet it gives you more than you have spent in return.

To be healthy, you must look closely at your energy investments. Where are you not getting your money's worth, and how can you turn your only outgoing or incoming lines into circles again? You're about to find out.

I would go so far as to say that this stop is the most important one on the road trip. Why? Because as the say-

Road Rule

The practice of health is the foundation for all your ultimate goals.

ing goes, if you have your health, you have everything. If you are in a positive inner balance, you will attract a positive balance of energy in all its forms: money, experiences, and relationships. Plus, you'll feel good enough to seize your opportunities when they are presented to you. You can't drive on empty, and it's hard to get going when you're sick.

To take a healing action is a big deal. It is to say, "Yes—I deserve to be alive and I deserve happiness and, moreover, I deserve to spend energy on making myself happy." This seems like a no-brainer, but, in fact, it can be a flash-point for the insecurities and fears you hold around your self-esteem.

To begin to accept healing, or inner balance into your life, is to honor yourself as precious, as someone who is worth all the love and energy of your most important relationships. That's a tall order, but now that you've been through the rest of the road trip, you are much more prepared to take this final step on your journey to care about—and for—your well-being as much as you would for anyone else.

Take a moment to write down any fears or limiting beliefs that come up when you think about beginning to move toward a more balanced lifestyle. Be honest—most of us say we want health, but there are deeper reasons that we still smoke, still drink, still become depressed, still give out way past our capacity. What are yours?

One of the major teachings of yoga and Buddhism is that when you orient your inner body—your consciousness—toward healing and happiness, that perspective will give you a positive experience of life, regardless of your external challenges. Some of the most miserable people I know have nothing physically wrong with them, and some with great health challenges spread joy wherever they go. Whether you can affect your physical being or not, you can change the degree to which you can enjoy your life and contribute meaningfully to society, by shifting the way you perceive all that is happening to you. Life only becomes suffering if you choose to make it so.

This philosophy is exemplified in Stephen Hawking, the scientist and mathematician who wrote *The Brief History of Time* and is one of the greatest minds of our, or any, generation. Hawking has an advanced case of Lou Gehrig's disease. He is wheelchair bound and uses a computer to speak, yet he has contributed an astounding amount of knowledge to our world.

I am not suggesting that by, using the information contained in this chapter Hawking will physically heal and begin to walk and talk on his own. But I am suggesting that no matter who you are, or what your physical issues are, you will benefit the most you possibly can from employing the principles found here at the magic gardens. Do you have a gift to give? I want to see you give it, as best you can.

There is the unavoidable fact that we all will die. Our physical bodies were not built to last forever—the soul, however, is a different story. I would rather you die close to your soul, with a smile on your face, from natural causes, next to your loved one after a full day of work and play, rather than falling prey to an avoidable disease.

Maybe your physical issues are reversible—maybe not. If you are sick, go to the doctor. If you are being prescribed medicine, you should take it. But our medical community is often one-sided. Many medicines only temporarily or artificially ease the symptoms, while the root causes remain untreated. I want you to get to the bottom of your health—not live in damage-control mode on the surface.

take the wheel
The Health Equation

To practice health and healing, you must know the health equation:

Life energy kept – Life energy spent = The state of your health

Like many profound teachings, this one looks easy but requires attention and vigilance to implement. Simply put, if you want to be healthier, you must always keep a surplus of life energy inside of you and not burn it all away. You learned this principle of nourishment while at the gas station. Now we'll take it a few steps further and show you how to keep your physical health invigorated. After all, you're on a road trip. You need your stamina.

Now You

What's your health equation right now? Write down all the ways you intake positive energy and what makes your energy drain out. How often does each happen to you during your day? Your week? Spend some time with this task and be specific. How often are you tired, stressed, or sick? How often do you feel energetic and balanced? What gets you to these places?

The energy intakes should outnumber the drains by far. No matter what your equation comes out to, here are some great ways to begin your practice of rebalancing it. Remember, do them often. Make each day into a healing ritual, and you will achieve a life that rewards you with vitality.

When realigning your actions to match your intentions to be healthier and enjoy a more abundant life, continually ask yourself the following two questions:

1. What can I do right now to benefit my health and healing goals?

2. What can I do next?

Having a healthy body, mind, and heart and/or engaging in consistent healing practices each day is a sign that you have stepped deeply into the currents of life and love. Daily health rituals are the signals that cause the rest of your reality to line up with what you desire. In the next section, I'll offer you some ideas on how to take better care of yourself. Some are simple; some require patience and discipline. All are powerful and originate from ancient principles of healing that have endured over centuries. Choose one or choose all, but leave very little room in your life for anything but creating health and denying disease any power over you.

What's on the Menu?

Say you are sitting down to dinner at a nice Italian restaurant. You look at the menu, and it's authentic southern Italian fare, made by a Sicilian chef. Would you look up at the waiter and say, "Do you have kung pao chicken?" No, because it's not even remotely on the menu. You wouldn't even think of asking. I want you to take this same concept and, with it, create a menu of your own. Instead of food, though, I want you to think in terms of healing items. The result will be your health menu.

What are those things that you can do, whether it's with your thoughts, emotions or actions each day, that bring you more good feelings inside and out—instead of less? Brainstorm, and write them all down. Even make menu-looking pages and have them available to look at when you're wondering what to do next for your health. If an action makes you feel happy, healthy, and strong on any one of your levels, put it on the menu. If it doesn't, you cannot "order" it—which means you can't think it, feel it, or do it. You must find ways to turn your poor-health diet into a nourishing one.

Anytime you feel off-track or embroiled in some stress or drama, turn right to your menu and order up some goodness—pronto! Here are a few ideas, straight from the actual health menus of some of my family members:

- Take rest stops. For every hour you expend energy or do something mindless, take a fifteen- to twenty-minute healing rest stop: a power nap, a meditation on something you love, or a restorative yoga pose (see my Web site for ideas).

- Call someone who loves and supports you.

- Pour a hot bath, and into it put lavender-scented essential oil and flower petals. Treat yourself like a queen while the water cleans and rebalances your energy.

- Take a hammering break. Find something that needs fixing, and fix it. It's preferable if this project includes hammering, drilling, or sawing loudly—literally constructive activity is a great stress reliever that brings a sense of accomplishment.

- Switch tracks. Take a deep breath and let it out slowly. Do this a few times and then decide to move your mind or body in another direction. Start a project, watch a good movie, or take a walk—anything you can concentrate on that's positive instead of letting the mind wander into the territory of disease.

Your menu will be longer—try for at least ten options. Put down things that inspire you, that will seem interesting and doable even when you're in a low mood.

Technical Support

If you need to lose weight, exercise more, or learn how to eat better, there is a whole world waiting for you that you may not have taken advantage of. The Internet has a vast amount of the latest information, ideas, and even chat and support groups made up of people just like you who are exchanging their old habits for more powerful ones. Here are places to start:

- PreventionMagazine.com
- ShapeMagazine.com
- FitnessMagazine.com
- Oprah.com
- DrPhil.com
- PodcastGo.com
- FoodNetwork.com
- I-Amplify.com
- iyogalife.com

At these sites, you will find articles, audio classes, forums, and video demonstrations for anything and everything healthy. Just go to any of them and start educating yourself about healing in one or more areas of your life. Out there in cyberspace, you'll find a warm, loving community devoted to giving you how-to advice and supporting your progress on everything from cooking well and working out to spirituality and relationship healing.

Go Green . . . or Go 5

If I could recommend only one change to your eating habits, it would be to make one of your meals each day a big health salad, a healing-in-a-bowl meal that will instantly increase your vitality while detoxifying your body and helping to prevent future illness. It might sound simple, but crafting a health salad that multitasks both nutrition and taste is an acquired art. Here are the basics and, once you know them, you can mix and match according to your tastes:

Your daily healing salad should include most of the following:

- Lettuce with a personality—not iceberg. Try red leaf, romaine, spinach, or mixed greens. Premade bags are quick and easy.

- At least five other colors. They can be fruit or veggies, but find bright, fresh ones and create a healing spectrum in your salad. I recommend radishes, red peppers, red onions, carrots, broccoli, blueberries, apple slices, tomatoes, mandarin oranges, corn, dried cranberries, asparagus, and shiitake mushrooms. All of these are incredible healers, and you can get so many of them to fit in just one meal.

- Protein power. Your body needs protein to repair and build muscles, among many other things. If you eat meat, try lean chicken, beef, fish, or turkey—sliced or cubed. If you don't, most beans, nuts, cheese (watch the fat), and tofu are great protein sources, too.

- Good fat. Your health salad isn't so healthy if you pour a bunch of calories and saturated fats over it, which many dressings contain. Either use much less, choose a healthier version, or make your own. Your body needs some fat to function properly, so don't fat-free yourself into a breakdown. Simply choose a natural dressing and use it sparingly. I make a tasty low-fat vinaigrette with a teaspoon of extra-virgin olive oil, one-quarter cup of Dijon mustard (stone ground or not), one-third cup of balsamic vinegar, a pinch of pepper, and a squeeze of fresh lemon. Whisk, and enjoy.

- Aim for organic. Whenever possible, choose organic and free-range, locally grown, small-farm foods. This way, as you heal yourself, you help to heal the world and support those who are working in harmony with it.

- Toss and enjoy!

Clean Up Your Cleaners

Your environment can make you sick or be a healing place. Replace your toxic, harsh cleaning supplies in the kitchen, bathroom, and laundry, and the products such as shampoos and lotions, that you put on your skin with chemical-free, healthy alternatives. Do you know that white vinegar and water is an excellent antibacterial cleaner? For easy recipes about how to make your own natural cleaning products, check out the book *The Naturally Clean Home: 100 Safe and Easy Herbal Formulas for Non-Toxic Cleansers* by Karyn Siegel-Maier.

Live Love

If you are in a job you hate, a relationship that deadens you, or any other soul-sucking situation, you must turn all your willpower, courage, and attention to moving away from those experiences. If you cannot distance yourself from the situation quite yet, find ways to balance and care for yourself as much as possible. I have had clients with scary, terminal diseases turn their illnesses around by radically transforming their jobs, their relationships, and their habits. When you demand joy from your life and leave yourself no other option but that, you have found the path to healing.

> *Never continue in a job you don't enjoy. If you're happy in what you're doing, you'll like yourself, you'll have inner peace. And if you have that, along with physical health, you will have had more success than you could possibly have imagined.*
>
> —JOHNNY CARSON

If your current reality is squeezing the life out of you, it is much more likely that you're going to start physically manifesting disease. Yet there is hope: reach out to friends, start putting feelers out for a new job, say no to abusive treatment in any form, and say yes to actions that are self-loving and choices that are true to your heart. If you can't leave your job right now, then start a book club, volunteer at a theater, or do whatever interests you.

Your time on this earth is short, and I invite you spend it living in love and healing in the process.

Get Thee to Yoga—Even Online!

I became enamored with this practice for a good reason: physical yoga is one of the only forms of exercise designed specifically to put life energy back into you, rather than drain it out. It's a powerful balancer of your hormones, brain, and central nervous system, which all help control your healing processes. Whether you're ill, well, a big muscle-bound guy, a superstretchy woman, or anything in between, if you find a style that is challenging to you without being overwhelming, yoga will tone, strengthen, and provide flexibility for your whole body, even as it energizes you. It's a complete healing circle!

If you find a yoga class or at-home sequence that's appropriate for you, and you work up to doing it for twenty to sixty minutes, three or more times per week, I guarantee you will notice a difference in your body, mind, and connection to your center. See my Web site for ideas.

Your Day as a Healing Art

Just as an artist sees a blank canvas, and on it begins to paint what he envisions, you look at the blank expanse of a day in front of you and decide what you wish to create of it. I invite you to take conscious strokes: let each action make your day into a work of healing art, which is to say that, no matter what anyone else is choosing to do, you will hold fast to your vision of someone who lives and breathes health.

You can begin to make a healing ceremony out of everything. Here are some ways I've found to transform a plain old day into a masterpiece:

- As you eat, follow the example of my Native American ancestors, and honor your food for giving you life. Thank it; pay attention to the meal and the moment at hand.

Chew slowly and notice the flavors. Imagine this food nourishing every cell of your body.

- Brew antioxidant-rich green or herbal tea in a beautiful pot, so you can enjoy pouring it during your own daily personal tea ceremony.

- Take a long bath, using candles, bath salts, and music. Water is energetically cleansing as well as soothing to the mind and body, and baths are long thought to have healing properties. Infuse the water with herbs or oils that promote the type of rebalancing you need.

- Sip lemon or cucumber/lime-infused water throughout the day, thinking about how it's rejuvenating you.

- Choose your words to express love instead of anger. If you feel bad after you've said something, apologize and try to communicate in a more understanding, calm way, even if you're talking to yourself.

- Edit your sensory input. Keep your exposure to mindless or negative TV, Internet, news, radio, or magazines to a minimum. Television is one of the most energetically draining devices in your home. The computer is next. So limit the amount of time you spend on them, especially if the time is not being used productively. Instead, fill your eyes, ears, heart, and soul with positive vibes: anything spiritual, interesting, or inspiring to you. Educate yourself about how to be a positive force in the world. Retrain yourself to be aware, but not overloaded with whatever is happening in the world, and remove that which is meaningless or pointlessly negative.

- Make a sleep paradise for napping and sleeping: low lights, sumptuous colors and fabrics, and comfortable sheets. If anything in the room jars you or causes mind clutter, remove it.

- Walk. Take a cue from Buddhist monks and do a short walking meditation, where you feel each step on the ground fully, even if it's only from your living room to the bedroom.

- Breathe. Pause sometimes to take deep inhales, filling up the space around your heart. Exhale for a little longer. Do this three times or more, for an instant peace-out moment and a burst of healing oxygen.

- Surround yourself with living things—plants, fish, pets, children, people, jogging trails, coffee shops—anything to bring you more fully into the current of being alive.

A Healing Spot

Create in your home a sacred space in which to sit each day and do your practices. This place is your healing spot. In feng shui, if every floor of your home was a perfect square, the health area would be right in the center, because health is the well from which all other areas of your life flow.

In the center of the ground floor of your home, or in the middle of any other room, create a healing spot. Find a way to place some life, such as a plant or fresh fruit, in or near the spot, or use anything that represents earth (for example, stones) and fire (candles, and the colors red and yellow). This way, you can have something to meditate upon when you're there and to attract healing energy when you're not.

Spend some time each day sitting in your spot, thanking yourself and the universal energy around you for the health you are receiving. It's important to make your gratitude into a present-tense mantra.

Maintaining a vital self is not an easy road, but it will become easier with time. The payoff of living on full power is that no matter what challenges or successes come your way, you will be able to meet them with a deep reservoir of life energy. You will have wasted very little energy on things that don't matter, so you can face the things that absolutely do with your whole presence.

These actions, and others you think up along the way, will help you reward yourself with good feelings and a sense of inner strength, which will become quickly more addictive than expending your energy on anything or anyone who does not give it back equally. Once you have healed all the way your spirit, the road home is wide open.

the final destination

Wishing You the Trip of a Lifetime

I Can See Clearly Now

As I write this, it's the morning after my LASIK eye correction surgery. I just finished going outside for a walk, and I marveled at the crispness of the clouds. Yesterday, I couldn't see the word *Pepsi* if I held the can out in front of me. I've worn glasses since I was eight, and the specs I thought were so cool back then have really begun to be a nuisance, especially in a downward-facing dog position.

When people asked if I was nearsighted or farsighted, I'd joke that my eyes were so bad I was insighted. I guessed I was meant to have more of an internal gaze than an external one in this life-time. Then I heard about this operation, and the doctor said I was a candidate, though off the charts as far as 20/20 vision went. I went blind for a few seconds in each eye during the procedure.

I thought, as the inevitable fear came, that maybe my path is not to see at all. But the doctor assured me this reaction was normal. I squeezed the blue rubber ball they gave me and breathed *ujjayi*.

After the procedure, which lasted about twenty minutes, the doctor sat me up and asked, "Can you tell me what time it says on the clock over there?" I looked at it, and instead of replying, "There's no way I can see that thing—it's too far away!" as I would have done ten minutes prior, I grinned and said, "It's 11:35."

I went home in a cab seeing as if underwater, and slept for hours with sunglasses on. When I awoke, I could see every title on my bookshelf—from ten feet away. Today, I can see the smallest line on the eye chart. I have 20/15 vision. The best part? For the first time ever, I clearly saw my life partner, Francis, in the doorway this morning as he readied to leave for work. He was smiling at me, and, I didn't miss it.

What was murky one day ago is now becoming clear. I still have to heal, and it's going to be a process of seeing more and more all the time—as you'll be doing on your road trip. Your final destination is also gaining full clarity, the eye-opening power to see yourself in all your glory: as the true, and ultimately, only creator of your life.

You Are Here

The final destination is also a location, and you know it well: it's wherever you find yourself, right now. The secret of the universe is that you've been in the exact right spot all along—to wake up and recognize that you have all you need to shine already within you. The road trip shows you how to illuminate that innate wisdom so you can find—and be—the soul of every place you stand.

Existing in full clarity is like looking around yourself and seeing that instead of being at a shopping mall, for example, you're a king or a queen standing in a hall of treasures, surrounded by angels. Every person you meet, book you read, thing you see, worldview you perceive, idea you contemplate, or choice you make is a chance to meet this true nature and live from your greatness. And ultimately, this is all you need to know.

Everything you thought you needed to reach out for is here right now—all you have to do is open your eyes.

Remember that Newton said, "For every action, there is an equal and opposite reaction." For you, the attractor of your intentions and manifestor of your dreams, this means that even as you look ahead in thought, word, and deed toward your ideals, you must just as fully draw inward, into the insight of exactly where you stand, and the answers that you already hold. Use the gifts of the present moment, and the action steps here in the road trip as your headlights, to help you discover the way ahead as you go.

When you realize that the soul of you is where everything begins, and where it all returns, you have made a core connection that will ground and sustain you no matter what—or whom—is coming or going externally. When you no longer blow around with the winds of change, yet can be flexible enough to allow the process to unfold, you have mastered the trip of your life.

It's a Two-Way Street

The road trip isn't a straight line. It's another power circle, but this one's special. The circle of your journey is like a two-lane roundabout. You're simultaneously traveling on the inside lane, reflecting within, listening and being, and you're driving on the outside, interacting, creating and doing. Yet as much as you'll perceive forward motion, you remain unmoved, existing both in the flow of traffic and sitting still in the driver's seat, knowing that nothing else needs to happen for you to be in love with your life—and everything you experience is a chance for you to find that love, that power, anew.

You are already on the path, and if you choose to do something, anything, it is just another creation that will have its consequences, but it does not waver the validity of your soul. There is no hurry to get anywhere, only to be more fully aware of *this* moment. In so doing, you will create your next moments of now in the mirror image of what you intended it to be. If you don't like what you've created, then change it—by changing your direction to bring you home again this instant.

So now, you can relax and be yourself. As you become used to the road you're on, you will notice more and more areas to refine each time you travel it.

It is my greatest hope that traveling this road trip, with me and all the other teachers gathered around you, has guided you to become clear about some important things you needed to remember. It's a vision quest; like all journeys of this nature, it begins by moving through the world and ends up back at the soul.

Am I exactly where I want to be? Yes and no. On my inner track, I'm content to be right where I am. Yet, I am also on the outer track and have a whole bunch of things I still want to accomplish and experience. My life has its challenges, too, and frustrating moments where I feel stuck. But today I'm clear: I see all these things that I'm passing through on my way toward my goals as learning experiences and chances to grow. I no longer allow them to remain as roadblocks to stop me. I keep rolling along, picking up more of myself all the way.

Slow Down

Do me a favor: resist the urge to do everything in this book at once. It will become an overwhelming task and is not even something I'd suggest. I have given you ideas, guidelines for the type of actions that can pay off for you. But if you try to do it all, you'll burn out. Keep it simple: pick a few of your favorites or create some of your own to begin turning into new habits, and add into your new lifestyle when you can.

Do you have to follow the road trip exactly in order to manifest your dreams? Absolutely not. Positive actions far outweigh negative ones, so when you do even one, you're overcoming tons of negativity. Aim for the majority of your time to be spent doing positive, conscious things. If you falter, stop yourself in your tracks, recommit to your road trip, and then relax about it. Leave missteps in the past, and besides, remind yourself that you're human.

The road trip should be fun, not a chore or a lackluster regimen. Maybe pick one thing from each stop to include each day, and aim for some more time-intensive ones during the week as you can. Make a checklist or a schedule, and see how you can comfortably fit it into your routine. If you feel like changing something, do it. Keep your road trip fresh, and you'll commit for longer until your new healing habits replace the outmoded ones.

Make It Yours

You can create your own road trip in the way that feels right to you. There are no rules, only my suggestion that you do more things that bring into your heart a feeling of sacredness, goodness, and love. When you choose; choose wisely, and all else will follow.

If you feel you need a tune-up in any area, go back through the book and make a stop again. Or do the whole road trip in its entirety. You will develop more clarity, more insight each time you do. Is the universe conscious? Does it know each of us personally, and when we ask for something, is it really thinking about us? I don't know. But I suspect that we each give the universe a little part of its consciousness, a bit of awareness as we invoke our inner power to resonate in the specific way we wish. Our personal frequencies all add up to a greater whole, one we can draw from as a creative source whenever we choose. So if we're it, then what we are, it also has to be—for each one of us, just as we stand.

In this scenario, as someone who has awakened and opened even a sliver of one eye in this new morning of your soul, you hold a great responsibility to help or hinder yourself, those around you, and the world community at large. You can make a change, by being what you're meant for, without apology or regret. I've given you all the reminders you need to help you to wake up and remember who you are and what you're here to do.

Now go and do it, be it, and, while you're at it, don't follow your dreams—*make* them happen.

If you'll excuse me, I'm going to pull off the road and go find a scenic outlook at which to look at my world through these brand-new eyes. You'll be fine on your own now, as you always were, and always will be. We'll meet again, I'm certain. For now, though, how about putting the pedal to the metal and leaving me in the dust. You've got a world of sightseeing to do.

See you on the road!

acknowledgments

I could not have created this book alone. Many souls have lent their eyes, ears, minds, hearts, and wisdom to the process, and their energies vibrate within these pages.

To my family and friends, who are the earth upon which I build my bonfires: Janet, Francis, Kris, Jay, Alex, Jen, Bari, and Ariel.

To my agents, Loretta Barrett and Nick Mullendore, for their unwavering vision and invaluable mentoring.

To the team at John Wiley & Sons and my editor, Tom Miller, for revealing the very heart of the trip from within.

Thank you to all my life's great teachers, whether the experience was beautiful or painful. You brought me home to myself, and I love you.

And last but not least, to every one of my students, readers, and viewers now and throughout the years. I could not do this work without you. You have given me a space into which to pour my soul. Thank you for bestowing the grace of your presence upon me no matter how briefly or how long the time we are together. It means the world.

May we each carry a living torch, feeding the flame through right action, knowing that all of us, following our own unique paths, will become illuminated along the way.

resources

For road-trip extras, Sadie's Core Strength DVD, yoga sequences, meditations, and more, visit www.sadienardini.com. Following are other recommended Web sites:

www.eastwestnyc.com, for my public classes, if you're in town

www.podcastgo.com, for quick and free video offerings from the pros, including my yoga podcasts

www.brentkessel.com, for balanced new ways to approach (and grow) your money

www.yogajournal.com, for a comprehensive yoga site

www.iyogalife.com, for an interactive healing community of spirit and my core-strength blog

www.thefengshuiguy.com, for contemporary feng shui ideas about realizing your intentions

www.shape.com, for a fitness and healthy eating extravaganza

www.freerice.com, for a fun way to feed the hungry right now, for free

www.childreninternational.org, to sponsor a child you'll come to love

recommended reading

Chodron, Pema. *The Places That Scare You: A Guide to Fearlessness in Difficult Times.* Boston: Shambhala, 2001.

Chopra, Deepak. *The Seven Spiritual Laws of Success: A Practical Guide to the Fulfillment of Your Dreams.* San Rafael, CA: Amber-Allen, 1994.

Cope, Stephen. *Yoga and the Quest for the True Self.* New York: Bantam Books, 1999.

Durgananda, Swami and Sally Kempton. *The Heart of Meditation: Pathways to a Deeper Experience.* South Fallsburg, NY: SYDA Foundation, 2002.

Huxley, Aldous. *Island.* New York: Perennial, 2002.

Nhat Hanh, Thich. *Anger: Wisdom for Cooling the Flames.* New York: Riverhead Books, 2001.

Orman, Suze. *The 9 Steps to Financial Freedom.* Philadelphia, PA: Miniature Editions, 2001.

Pressfield, Stephen. *The War of Art: Break through the Blocks and Win Your Inner Creative Battles.* New York: Warner Brothers, 2002.

Roach, Geshe Michael. *The Diamond Cutter: The Buddha on Managing Your Business and Your Life.* New York: Doubleday, 2000.

Surya Das, Lama. *Awakening the Buddha Within: Eight Steps to Enlightenment: Tibetan Wisdom for the Western World*. New York: Broadway Books, 1997.

Walsch, Neale Donald. *Home with God: In a Life That Never Ends: A Wondrous Message of Love in a Final Conversation with God*. New York: Atria Books, 2006.

index